Poems chiefly written in retirement. The Fairy of the Lake, a dramatic romance; Effusions of Relative and Social Feeling; and specimens of the Hope of Albion, or Edwin of Northumbria; an epic poem. With a prefatory Memoir of the life of the author.

John Lecturer. Thelwall

Poems chiefly written in retirement. The Fairy of the Lake, a dramatic romance; Effusions of Relative and Social Feeling; and specimens of the Hope of Albion, or Edwin of Northumbria; an epic poem ... With a prefatory Memoir of the life of the author and notes and illustrations of Runic mythology. (Second edition.).

Thelwall, John Lecturer.
British Library, Historical Print Editions
British Library
1801.
8°.
1465.f.7.(2.)

The BiblioLife Network

This project was made possible in part by the BiblioLife Network (BLN), a project aimed at addressing some of the huge challenges facing book preservationists around the world. The BLN includes libraries, library networks, archives, subject matter experts, online communities and library service providers. We believe every book ever published should be available as a high-quality print reproduction; printed on- demand anywhere in the world. This insures the ongoing accessibility of the content and helps generate sustainable revenue for the libraries and organizations that work to preserve these important materials.

The following book is in the "public domain" and represents an authentic reproduction of the text as printed by the original publisher. While we have attempted to accurately maintain the integrity of the original work, there are sometimes problems with the original book or micro-film from which the books were digitized. This can result in minor errors in reproduction. Possible imperfections include missing and blurred pages, poor pictures, markings and other reproduction issues beyond our control. Because this work is culturally important, we have made it available as part of our commitment to protecting, preserving, and promoting the world's literature.

GUIDE TO FOLD-OUTS, MAPS and OVERSIZED IMAGES

In an online database, page images do not need to conform to the size restrictions found in a printed book. When converting these images back into a printed bound book, the page sizes are standardized in ways that maintain the detail of the original. For large images, such as fold-out maps, the original page image is split into two or more pages.

Guidelines used to determine the split of oversize pages:

• Some images are split vertically; large images require vertical and horizontal splits.
• For horizontal splits, the content is split left to right.
• For vertical splits, the content is split from top to bottom.
• For both vertical and horizontal splits, the image is processed from top left to bottom right.

EX 1

THE FAIRY

OF

THE LAKE.

A Dramatic Romance.

IN THREE ACTS.

Characters.

ROWENNA, *Queen of Britain; a Sorceress.*
EDELTHRED, *and* AGGA, *Her attendants*
ALWIN, *a Saxon Chief.*
SENESCHAL.
SEWER.
A BRITISH NOBLE, *attendant on the Court of Vortigern.*
SAXON NOBLES, SOLDIERS, and other attendants.

ARTHUR, *the British Champion.*
TRISTRAM, *his Esquire.*
SCOUT, *another Esquire.*
TALIESSIN, *Chief of the Bards.*
GUENEVER, *Daughter of Vortigern, betrothed to Arthur.*
BARDS, KNIGHTS of the Round Table, NOBLES, MASKERS, &c.

THE FAIRY (or LADY) of THE LAKE.
Several FAIRIES, &c. her attendants.

HELA, *Queen of the Infernal Regions.*
INCUBUS, *a frozen demon.*
URD,   *The Fatal Sister presiding over*   the past.
VERANDI,   the present
SCHULDA,   the future.
THE GIANTS OF FROST; DEMONS of the Frozen Regions; DEMONS of the Noon, &c. &c.

THE FAIRY OF THE LAKE.

ACT I. SCENE I.

A Stately Appartment in one of the Palaces of VORTIGERN.

ROWENNA *reclining in a difconfolate attitude.* EDELTHRED, AGGA, *and other Attendants fleeping.*

CHORUS OF INVISIBLE SPIRITS.

ROWENNA rife!   Thy beauteous eyes
  From clouds of forrow clear;
With Runic fpell   Each woe repel,
  And dry the falling tear.
Semi cho. Rowenna ! pride of Woden's race !
  With fovran power, with beauty's grace,
    And magic numbers bleft !
  The impaffive fpirits of the air
  Obedient round thy couch repair,
    To footh the troubled breaft.
Cho. Rowenna rife ! &c.
Semi cho. Thee, Chauntrefs of the Runic fong !
  The mifty Realms of Froft among,
    The fhuddering ghofts obey.

Sem. cho. Thy power the Fatal Sisters own,
And Hela, trembling on her throne,
Admits thy potent sway.

Cho. Rowenna, rise, &c.

Sem. cho. For thee Valhalla's halls are mute;
Nor Wassail bowl, nor dire dispute
The warrior chiefs employ.

Sem. cho. While Frea, from Asgardian bowers,
No more among her votaries showers
The genial shafts of joy.

Cho. Rowenna rise! Thy beauteous eyes
From clouds of sorrow clear:
With Runnic spell Each woe repel,
And dry the falling tear.

ROWENNA *(rushing forward with great emotion.)*

Arthur!—Arthur!—Hence, away,
Intrusive spirits of the air;
Nor, with officious zeal, display
How impotent immortal care.

Sem. cho. Hear, Rowenna!—Mistress hear!

Row. Arthur!—Arthur!—In my heart
I feel—I feel the festering dart:
'Tis Arthur!—Arthur! all.
In vain Asgardia's sacred bowers,
In vain Valhalla's shield-built towers,
Asori's gods, and Hela's powers
Their mission'd daughter call.

Sem. cho. Hear, Rowenna!—Mistress, Hear!

Sem. cho. Still thy bosom. Dry the tear.

Sem. cho. Snatch thy wand !—
    Sem. cho. Exert thy power !
Sem. cho. O'er Afgard's foes triumphant tower,
  And chace the troubled tear.
Cho. And chace the troubled tear.
Row. Arthur !—Arthur !—Hence— away,
  Intrufive fpirits of the air,
  Nor mock me with officious care.
In vain did Frea charms beftow,
And Schulda o'er the realms below
  To rule with runic fpell.
In vain with Braga I repeat,
In myftic rhyme, Afamael fweet,
  And tune the immortal fhell.
In vain by me the Saxon name
O'er proftrate Britain towers to fame.
  Myfelf inglorious fall.
The conquering fword—the magic art
Are baffled by the apoftate heart.
  'Tis Arthur !—Arthur all.

Yes—yes—'tis fruitlefs. Minifter no more,
Ye ever-hovering fpirits ! 'tis in vain,
To footh this ftorm-tofs'd bofom. Earth and Air,
And the deep-bofom'd waters, to this wand,
Indeed, pay homage; and the elfin train
That round the harp of Braga, echoing, throng
(Swelling his magic numbers) on my fteps
Wait warbling; and with minftrelfey and voice,
Obedient to my wifhes, fill the air

With choral melodies. My wiley arts
Have thrall'd the foul of Vortigern; in whom
Britain, my foe, lies proftrate; and the gods
Of Scandinavia in my witching fmiles
Build their enfanguin'd altars. Cambria's fons,
And all the Brutean race, already feel
The woman victor. Even the nether world,
Seafons, and circling Elements obey
My potent biddings. Cloud-compelling Thor
Muft wield his thundering Gauntlet, or controul,
With lifted Mace, the Giants of the Froft
If I but chaunt The Rhyme. Yet what avails?
Arthur difdains my charms; and o'er his heart,
My fpells are powerlefs. Yet once more I'll try.
Once more the fecret dwellings of The Fates
This ken fhall pierce. Thefe feet again fhall thrid
The abodes of Hela.   Rife, ye miniftering maids,
Shake from your flothful lids the charmed fleep,
And do your wakeful fervice.   [*They come forward.*
            Edelthred!
Haft thou heard aught of ftrange or terrible
Marring thy midnight flumber?
        Edelthred. Nothing, Madam.
My fleep was fweet and tranquil.
        Row. Well—and yours?
  Agga. Full of fweet vifions—gentle and ferene.
  Row. 'Twas as I wifh'd. Oh! impotence of power!
Terreftrial, or fupernal! To each eye—
All but mine own—to every wearied fenfe
My fpells can give fweet flumber; from my lids
While reftlefs Anguifh drives the balmy Sylph,

Or Mara from fome brief imperfeȼt dream
Wakes me, delirious, on her phantom'd forms
To gaze with powerlefs horror.   'Tis too much.
Hell, give me more: or take the power ye gave.
Give me to triumph o'er my Arthur's heart,
And in thefe arms enfold him! or my fpells,
Hence I forfwear, this gifted wand I break,
Nor at the altars of Afgardian Gods
Chaunt hence the Runic rhyme.

       Hafte Edelthred;
Bring here my myftic robes: the fame that erft
(While the dire Sifters join'd the fearful chaunt)
I wove in Cimbrian groves.

    Air *by an invifible Spirit.*

   Magic Woof, in Cimbrian fhade
   Woven by the gifted maid,
   While the Raven-voice of Fate
   Croak'd of flaughters, fears, and hate,
Sem. cho. Shuddering Horror liftning near.
Row. 'Tis the fame.   Go : bring it here.
    Air *as before.*
   There, beneath the blafted yew,
   Where reptiles lap the poifonous dew,
   While the bird who fhuns the day
   Hooted loud, and tore his prey—
Semi cho. There 'twas wove—a webb of fear!
Row. Its die it drank from infant gore,
   And tears of mothers blotch it o'er;
   Groans from its ruftling folds refound,
   And hiffing ferpents fringe it round.

It is a myſtic webb of fear.
Haſte my virgins : bring it here.

Ed. Hertha defend! What means our troubled Queen?
Row. Again, in that terrific pall, to thrid
The maze of Hela; and with potent rhyme,
Extort a boon from Fate.   Can I controul
The tempeſt-heaving Nocca? at my will
Brandiſh the Thunderer's gauntlet? rend the air
With bidden ſtorms? and from the ſhades of night
Evoke the wandering ſpirit? yet not quench,
With its deſir'd fruition, the fierce flame
That preys upon my vitals?   Does the power
Of magic numbers not extend to Love?
Or are our gods faſtidious, to deny
An unbelieving paramour?—ſave ſuch
Whom Weakneſs to uxorious faith may bow:
Pageants! and Vortigerns!   My Pall! My Pall!
   By that dread Fiend Unutterable! whoſe frown
Makes Nature ſterrile, I will know my doom.
The Fatal Siſters, who, in Hela's ſhade,
Weave the dark woof, ſhall tell me all they know,
And with their magic aid me.   Yet—forbear!
Earth and the ſhuddering elements confeſs
The approach of feet profane.
                    Edel. The bugle (hark!)
Wakening the echoes, thro the diſtant courts
Sounds in the hurried blaſt.
                    Row. Some voice, aſſured,
Of evil omen ſeeks my wounded ear,

Big with a tale of horrors. Let it come.
What worfe can greet Rowenna than the news
That Arthur fcorns her paffion?

Enter ALWIN.

       Well: how now?
Thy dark portentous brow and hurried eye
Outftrip thy tongue's intelligence, and make
Thy filence eloquent. Thou haft fome tale
Of horrors and difafters. Give it breath.
I have a heart prepar'd for all the worft:
A foul that fhall not falter. I forgive
Thy evil tidings, tho they fhould import
My father's death, the Saxon overthrow,
And Cambria's triumph.

      Alwin. Prophetefs infpired!
Thy words prevent my meffage. Such my news.
Hengift, indeed, is fallen: The Saxon power
Crouches to Britain. To the conflict led
By fierce Ambrofius, with Armoric aids,
Sudden they burft upon us, near the towers
Of Connifburg. Arthur's enchanted fword
Gleam'd like a peftilence; and thro' our ranks
Scatter'd difmay and death. His dragon creft
Belch'd ftreams of living fire; and on his breath
The dread Valkyries hung; where'er he bad,
Singling their victims.

      Row. Arthur? Arthur?

        Alw. He—
Pendragon's fiercer fon. In horrid grace,

B

Wrathful he ftrode the field.   His glittering mail
And youthful limbs, befmear'd with Saxon blood,
Daz'd every fenfe.   With awful wonder fill'd,
Our hearts were palfy'd: as tho Woden's felf,
Frefh from Iduna's banquet, came renew'd,
To ply the work of Fate, and his own race
Whelm in one general wreck.   Meantime the king,
· Your royal father———

    Row. Met his arm; and died?——
By Arthur died?

   Alw. Not fo——That fatal deed
Ambrofius boafts——who, hoary in his hate,
And full of guile, engor'd with treacherous wound
The elfe-engaged Hengift: and he fell——
Fell by the Briton!——while our fcatter'd ranks
Fled o'er the plain for fafety——vainly fought.

  Row. Frea! I thank thee.   Genial Goddefs! hail!
Hail the propitious omen!   'Twas thy care
That Hengift's blood ftain'd not the hand of Arthur.

  Purfue thy tale.   Some other hour, more fit,
We will feleĉt for tears.   Occafions prefs;
And we muft find prompt councils.   Whether fled
The abjeĉt Vortigern?

    · *Alw.* From bourg to bourg
(By all alike rejeĉted) with his fuit,
Weftward he fled, towards his Cambrian wilds, ·
A hunted fugitive: till join'd, at laft,
By thofe who 'fcap'd the flaughter, he attain'd
The heights of bleak Farinioch. . There he lurks,
Hem'd by Gwrtheyrnion's towers, whofe giant ftrength

Frowns o'er the midway fteep.   Thither he bore
(From his inceftuous paffion uneftrang'd)
His fair, reluctant daughter, Guenever.

 Row. She fcap'd not then into the arms of Arthur?
She is fecure.   Revenge at leaft is fure:
And Love has hope! Say, haft thou aught befide
That may import my hearing?

     Alw. Sovereign! nought:
But that the exulting victor, to deftroy
The Saxon hope, has purpofe to depofe
Our pageant Vortigern; and, in his place,
Crown the new idol, Arthur.

    Row. (*afide*) Arthur crown'd?
And fo he fhall be.   But not crown'd by them.
That is Rowenna's Dower: the dower confirm'd
By the three Fatal Sifters.—While I live,
Thy empire, Albion, waits my fpoufal love:
And Arthur, if he reigns, muft reign by me.
Alwin, what elfe?

    Alw. Your royal will.   Befide
Nought now remains untold.

    Row. Then, Alwin, thus—
Hafte to Gwrtheyrnion with what fcatter'd powers
Your fpeed may gather.   See the gates fecur'd
Againft my foon arrival.   I fhall bring
Such powerful fuccours as may beft defend
The alpine fortrefs, fhould the victors dare
To prefs us to a fiege. Away.   Begone. [*Exit Alw.*

 O Edelthred! O Agga! why fhould thus
My heart beat lighter, and the breath more free

Diſtend my ſportive boſom ? Hengiſt ſlain—
The Saxon routed !—Here is cauſe of grief
For Nature and Ambition. But my ſoul
Is full of Love and Arthur. Frea ſmiles
To my beſt hopes propitious ; and, amidſt
The ſtorms of adverſe deſtiny, my heart
Finds anchor in her aid.

        Goddeſs of the genial hour !
           Hear, O ! hear my votive ſigh ;
       And, tho' adverſe Fortune lour,
           Fear and Sorrow I defy,
              Goddeſs of the genial hour !
       Grief may drop the tranſient tear,
           Wild Ambition heave the breaſt ;
       But, if thou in ſmiles appear,
           All is tranquil—all is bleſt,
              Goddeſs of the genial hour !
       Fear and Sorrow I defy,
           Tho my adverſe fortune lour,
       Hear but thou my votive ſigh,
           Goddeſs of the genial hour !

Edel. And ſhe will hear it—if we aught may judge
The future by the preſent. Could we hope
A fairer pledge of promiſe ? Arthur's hand
Slew not your father.—Arthur's conquering aid
Could not redeem his Guenever.
                Row. 'Tis there
My fondeſt hopes are fix'd.—Still, ſtill ſhe pines

In hoſtile bonds—ſtill hears with ſteadfaſt hate
(Would it were not ſo ſteadfaſt!) the foul ſuit
Of that inceſtuous Vortigern : or writhes,
Perchance, ſubjeſted to his foul embrace,
Calling, in vain, on Arthur.   I will aid
The lawleſs paſſion of this monſter king,
Goading his vile deſires, and urging on
To their impell'd fruition.   Haply ſo
(For man, with ſickly appetite, abhors
Oft from the trick of Fancy) Arthur hence
Shall loath her rifled beauties : She no more
Shall ſeem or chaſte or lovely ; and his eyes
Confeſs ſuperior merit.   Then ſhall ſoon
Adultrous Vortigern my vengeance feel;
And his polluted paramour : This hand
Shall lift my Arthur to an envied throne,
And our united ſceptres blend the tribes
Of Cimbria and of Britain.   Say I well?
    Agga. Well : if The Fates ordain,
                          Row. We will enquire.
And for ſuch purpoſe in The Secret Grove
Chaunt we the ſpell.   My double-viſag'd Fate
(Ghaſtly at once and jocund) goads me on
Amidſt a ſtorm of paſſions.   To The Grove
Initiate Virgins, and the haunted cave ;
There join the fearful chaunt.   And ye, unſeen—
Ye ſhapeleſs ſpirits of the impaſſive air,
Lend me your minſtrelſey.   Yet firſt evoke
The oafiſh Incubus.   While yet the bat,
Beneath the ominous mantle of the night,

Follows the beetles hum, be it his tafk
To fcout the country round; if chance he learn
Tidings of Arthur; who, at once impell'd
By love and by ambition, will purfue
The fteps of Guenever. Him fhould he find,
Upon the attendant train let him effay
His numbing tricks: that while they, fhivering, fink
In fenfelefs torpor, Arthur, all alone
Thefe eyes once more may meet. Evoke the fiend.
What further I defign the myftic grove
And fecret cave fhall witnefs. Join me there
Where, in my Cimbrian pall and fnaky tire,
I chaunt the fpell to Hertha.

Howl of wolves, and ghofts of night,
In the fearful chorus join,
While The Moon withdraws his light,
And the ftars, in dim afright,
Veil their orbs, and fear to fhine.
Hark!—they wait to fwell the rite—
Howl of wolves and ghofts of night!

[*Exeunt* Row. Edel. *&c.*

SCENE II. *Manet* Agga,

Agga. Incubus! Incubus!

Incubus, (*below.*) Whu-u-u! Whe-e-ether now?
Wh-o-o calls fo loud?

Agga. You know, I trow.
Incubus! Incubus!
Did you not your Miftrefs hear?

Incub. Ye-e-e-e-yes—

Behold your fhivering devil here.

*The ground unclofes, and thro the chafm rifes a mea-
gre fpectre, with a blue and frofty countenance,
funken eyes, frozen locks and beard, and garments covered with icicles.*

Incub. (Shaking the fnow from his fides.) Whu-u-u-u!

What's the bufinefs pr'ythee now?

Agga. Son of Froft! you know I trow.

Did you not your Miftrefs hear?

Incub. Hear? O yes; there's no fear of that, I
affure you. When 'tis a woman we ferve, our orders
are fure to be fufficiently audible! The frofts of Hela
cannot plug up one's ears againft the *clear* tones of
the feminine organ. But pr'ythee now, leave off your
rhyming and your incantations, and blow my fingers
for me a little.—It is half a century fince I have
been able to breathe any thing but fleet and hailftones
upon them myfelf.

Agga. Really I have no warm breath to fpare upon fo
cold a fubject.

Incub. Why I fuppofe, indeed, I am not very engag-
ing. Some thoufand years hence, when ice-creams are
predeftined to become an article of luxury, fome lady
of honour, may chance to take a liking to a joint or
two, by way of ftomachic: But at prefent, I believe,
there is no great danger of my being devour'd by
the fair fex.

Agga. Not if they are of my tafte, at leaft.

Incub. But pray, good Mrs. Journeywoman Sorcerefs! have you any further inftructions? Any fnug little commiffion for yourfelf?

Agga. Good Mr. Journeyman Devil! no.—If ever
I admit any of your infernal train into my fervice, it
fhall be a devil of better quality.

Incub. Aye! aye! Mrs. You are for a good plump
roafting Devil I fuppofe. This effence of fnow and
icicles might melt before the blaze of your beauty.

Agga. What, you think I have fome attractions then?

Incub. Attractions! Before I defcended into the regions of Hela, to have my blood converted into icicles,
I fhould have been ready to die for you any half hour
of my exiftence.

Ag. Were you fuch a Dragon amongft us in your
life time?—Come, come; I fufpect it was not for this
you were fent to The Frozen Regions

Inc. Why, no: offences of that fort are punifhed in
a Hell of a very different defcription. In fhort, there
is no diffembling. You know the myfteries of our
faith; and the thing fpeaks for itfelf. Our fifticuff
Divinities and I happened not to fet up our horfes
together on the fubject of the exquifite delight of being
hacked and hewed into a thoufand pieces. Not
but that I could be valiant enough in my own way!
for my mouth was full of big oaths; and my brow
feemed as dark with danger as a thunder-cloud: till a
difaftrous coincidence took the fword of my renown
out of my mouth, and placed it in my hand.

Ag. Ha! ha! poor Incubus! And then I fuppofe

it was perfectly out of its element.

Inc. In fhort, the fignal for battle was given; when fuddenly a cold fweat coming over me, I flunk from the ranks; hid myfelf in a houfe of conveniency; died of apprehenfion, before the conflict was decided; was conveyed immediately to the Realms of Mift and Froft, and hung up for an icicle upon the eaves of Hela's palace; where I might right ruefully have remained, without remiffion or intermiffion, hope or holiday, the whole prediftinated period of my purgation.——

Agga. Purgation? What, then, you do not expect to await The Twilight of the Gods in your prefent frozen ftate?

Incub. Schulda forbid! Let me fee, according to my calculation, I have now——But if your invifible muficians will help me out with an accompaniment, I will defcribe, in a fong, the year of my regeneration.

When the twelvemonth's contention of Cent'ries is done,
Whether eighteen be ended, and nineteen begun,
And Learning and Science their optics fhall ftrain
To find fome new nothing to puzzle the brain;
Then the Fates to this world fhall my effence reftore,
To fhudder in Regions of Hela no more.

O! how different the race that my eyes fhall behold!
For a foul of my kidney a true age of Gold!
Since none for his fears can be look'd on the worfe,
Where they count for their fame not their fears but their purfe

    Then the Fates to this World, &c.

Then The Fair--Oh! how fair their sweet persons will shine,
When our helmets and scull-caps to them we resign,
When no grace of the form shall in vain be bestow'd,
And nakedness self be the tip of the mode.

Then their motions so easy, their manners so free!
In *ferae naturae* you'd deem them to be;
And Miss just in her teens, from all bashfulness freed,
Shall now skip o'er the rope, and now skip o'er the tweed:

O! how gay then I'll flirt and I'll flutter around,
Where the belles of the young 19th Cent'ry are found!
Their charms so obtrusive shall kindle a flame,
Shall melt all the ice that now stiffens my frame;
And I'll think, while Love's ardour shall glow in each pore,
Of the Regions of Frost and of Hela no more.

[*Exeunt.*

*SCENE III. The Magic Grove; with the entrance of
the Cave of Incantations—a rude and rocky chasm,
overhung with shattered yew trees, and every specie
of gloomy and noxious vegetation. The darkness of
the scene is only imperfectly interrupted by the transient
glare of meteors from above, and the blue vapours, or
fen damps, that play about the Magic Circle described
at the entrance of the Cave. Shrieks and groans, and
bellowing noises, heard occasionally in the air; &c.*

ROWENNA *is discovered, arrayed in her Pall and snaky
Tiara;* EDELTHRED *and others attending; their*

hair difhevelled, and intermixed with Ivy, Hemlock, Nightfhade, &c. A Female Child *accompanies them, bearing the Pictured Drum and Double Hammer, with a rofary of Brazen Rings, and images of ferpents, frogs, toads, and other obfcene reptiles, ufed in the myfteries of Northern Magic.*

Row. Strike, ftrike, The myftic Drum, virgin yet pure
Of paffion's fecret wifh! from facred folds
Of chill equatic Loomfkin, lift on high
The awful Hammer, while the Brazen Ring,
Viper, and venom'd Toad, and Frog that croaks
In pools obfcene, and Newt of mouldering wall
Dance o'er the pictur'd furface, and in reel
Prophetic of our wavering deftinies,
Lead up The Rites.
      Ye Demons of the Storm!
Who thro the mirky clouds with tranfient glare
Stoop to our incantations, or, appall'd,
Shriek in the midnight blaft, with yell or groan
Swelling the chorus of the fhuddering Grove,
While growls the diftant bear, and in his den
The hungry wolf barks fear-chain'd!—it is well;
Ye feel my power, and own it. Aid me then
In thefe myfterious Rites—or ye who rive
With Thor's own bolts the groaning earth, or ye
Who to the labouring mine's combuftion'd womb
Dart the contagious fpark, whence Earthquake rends,
Or pent Volcano fpits his fulphurous fires,
Wide wafting! for to Hela's mifty realms

I force my way, and to The Fatal Three
Who weave the Webb of Deſtiny. [*Enter* AGGA.
　　　　　　　　How now ? —
Tardy and ſhuddering? Haſt thou in thy way
Gather'd the ſpume-froth'd drugs, on which, o'ertoil'd,
The Bat hath crouch'd, and the Night-Swallow drop'd
Her half-churn'd morſels ?—

　　　Agga. Miſtreſs, they are here :—
But, uſe them not! Some hoſtile ſtar prevails—
Our Gods forſake us. Never, ſince the hour
When, with initiate feet, I firſt approach'd
This myſtic Circle, felt my ſoul ſuch horror.
At ever and anon, as, from my ſpeed
Pauſing, I ſtoop'd, ſome ominous ſhriek was heard,
Or deathlier groan :—the herbs, o'erconſcious, ſhrunk
My trembling touch; the glare of fiery eyes
Peep'd from the unhallow'd turf; and up mine arm
Darts the benumbing ſhock—as lightning ſtruck!—
That three-times thrice (while ſhook the earth beneath)
From my full apron drop'd the unwilling ſtore—
With ſhuddering toil replac'd. Forbear! forbear
The ill-omen'd ſpell!

　　　Row. Mere womaniſh fear. Away!
My ſoul is all on fire, and I muſt ſeek
The quenching ſtream, or periſh. Come: draw near.
Give me The Drugs. Thus from my bruiſing hands
I preſs the powerful dews. Now, ſtrike again
The ſpheric Drum, and in the fawn's warm blood
Stoop, ſtoop and waſh—'Tis done. Begin the chaunt.

Chorus. Hela! hear!

Edel. Queen of Niflheim's misty shade

Agga. Frozen Hela! ghastly maid!

Row.   From thy Throne of Horrors—hear!

Edel. By the Giants of the Frost!

Agga. By Ifing's fury-beaten coast!

Row.   By thy Dome of Anguish—hear!

Edel. By thy Table, Famine-spread!

Agga. By thy lean unshelter'd Bed!

Row. Threshold bleak and Chasm dread!

  Chorus. Hela! hear!

Edel. Furies dread of Woden's hall!

Agga. By whom the fated heroes fall—

Row.   Dread Valkyries!—bend and hear!

Edel. And ye Nornies—fearful three!

  Who thro Fate's dark workings see—

   Weaving the Webb that mortals fear—

  Chorus. Fatal Sisters! list, and hear!

Row. bending towards the earth, with her Wand up-
   lifted, as in act to strike.

  Hertha! ope thy rock-rib'd side—

  Ribs of Ymer's giant pride!

  Ribs by Odin, Vile, and Ve—

  Awful Godhead! mystic Three!

  From Ymer torn, and giv'n to thee.

Adel. and Agga. Hertha! ope thy rock-rib'd side—

  Ribs of Ymer's giant pride!

  Chorus. Hertha! hear!   [*A groan below.*

Edel. Hertha labours.   Soon the fpell
      Shall her reluctant womb compel.
Agga. Soon the once-tried depths below
      Again their gates fhall open throw.

Row.   Ceafe, ye maidens—ceafe your ftrains:
      Mine the tafk that yet remains.
      Hertha's rock-rib'd fide unclofes;
      Hell its hideous womb expofes;
      Groans, and fhrieks, and plaints of woe
      Roar in troubled floods below.
      Fly ye maids!   To me alone
      Hertha's fecret ways are known.

Subterranean thunder. EDELTHRED, AGGA, *&c. difappear. The cavern burfts open. A fwarm of hideous*
PHANTOMS *rufh, with great clamour, from the cleft;
thro whom* ROWENNA *rufhes, and defcends. The*
PHANTOMS *form themfelves into groups, fome of
which join in a fort of fantaftic and conflicting dance,
ftriking at each other, and buffetting the air; while
others join in difcordant chaunt.*

Chorus.   Fell enchantrefs! hold! forbear!
1. *Phantom.* 'Tis in vain.   We beat the air.
2. *Ph.*   Phantom'd Terrors glare in vain.
3. *Ph.*   Nature's laws no more reftrain.
All three.   Defperate Magic burfts the chain.
Cho.   Hertha groans in terrene thunder:
      Ribs of rock are burft afunder.

1. *Ph.*	Sulphur! 2. *Ph.* Nitre! 3. *Ph.* Miner's damp,
	Fatal to the vital lamp—
All.	Thro the cavern'd entrails fume:
2. *Ph.*	And the Wolf-like Serpent's fpume.
Chorus.	Midgard's Serpent, fierce and dread,
	Lifts his all-devouring head.
1. *Ph.*	Fiercely writhes his fcaly zone.
2. *Ph.*	Nature trembles on her throne.
Cho.	Gods and Hela join the groan.
1. *Ph.*	Hark! the Hell-dog's tripple growl!
2. *Ph.*	Rafaen's fcream! 3. *Ph.* And Fenrir's howl!
Cho.	Thrilling fhriek! and deaf'ning growl!
1. *Ph.*	Fell enchantrefs! 2. *Ph.* On fhe goes—
3. *Ph.*	Eager of impending woes.
All.	To the nine-fold realm fhe goes!

CHORUS.

Hertha's rock-rib'd fide unclofes;
Niflheim's gloom in vain oppofes;
Groans, and fhrieks, and plaints of woe
Roar, in bootlefs floods, below.

They rufh into the chafm, and it clofes.

SCENE IV. The Abodes of Hela.

*The Stage, at firft, appears involved in darknefs and mift,
    fo that the objeEls at the back part of the fcene are not dif-
    cernable. Thunder and occafional flafhes of Lightning.*

Row. (without). Hela!—Hela!—Hela!
Hela. What mortal organs thus aloud proclaim,
    With tripple invocation, Hela's name?

Row. (entering) Regent of the nine-fold fhade!
 Shuddering Hela! Ghaftly Maid!
 Bid the mifts of darknefs fly
 Scattering from the nether fky!

Hela. Say who art thou who thus, with daring tread,
Invad'ft the dreary manfions of the dead ?

  Fear! prefumptuous mortal! fear!
  Draw not to my threfhold near.
  Draw not near! Confefs thy fear!
  And fhun my fury ere too late.
Row. Hela! no:—I cannot fear ;
 Tho the Furies all appear,
  Sprung from Lok's prolific hate.
Hela. Draw not near. Learn to fear
  Fenrir's howl, and Hela's hate.
Row. Hela, no : I cannot fear
  Fenrir's howl, or Niflheim's hate.

  By the channels twelve that drank
  Hevergelmer's vapours dank,
  Where the direful rivers flow,
  Streams of horror, plaint, and woe !
  I have travers'd, void of fear,
  To feek the Fatal Sifters here.

Cho. Regent of the nine-fold fhade!
 Shuddering Hela! Ghaftly Maid!
 Bid the mifts of darknefs fly.

Row.   O'er the Bridge where Giöl rolls—
         Fearful pafs to daftard fouls!
         By The Dog of hideous yell,
         By the iron grate of Hell;
         Ghaftly Hela! I have come
          To tax The Fates, and know my doom.

Cho.   Regent of the nine-fold fhade!
         Shuddering Hela! ghaftly Maid!
         Bid the mifts of darknefs fly.

     Trio, and Chorus, by The Fatal Siflers, &c.
Urd and ⎱   Who art thou who thus prefume
Schulda. ⎰   To tax the Fatal Siflers o'er their loom?
Verandi. Fly! daring-mortal!
Urd.   Daring mortal! fly.
Schulda.   Fly! nor urge thy inftant doom.
Cho. Fly, daring mortal! fly: nor urge thy inftant doom!

Row.   Hela! from thy nether fky
         Bid the mifts of darknefs fly:
         Soon fhall to your eyes appear
         One your fhuddering fpeêtres fear.
         Soon The Siflers o'er the loom
  The fhuttled hand fhall check, and tell my doom.

         Hela, from the nether fky
         Bid the mifts of darknefs fly,
         Ere the loud refiftlefs fpell
         Shake the dire abodes of Hell—

D

Ere this wand's terrific ſtroke
The Unutterable Fiend evoke.

Hela. Fly! ye miſts of Nörver—fly!—
Dager claims our nether ſky.
Dread Enchantreſs! ſtop the ſpell.
Rowenna!!!——Now I know thee well.

The miſts diſperſing, HELA *is diſcovered; a meagre
ghaſtly ſpeĉtre, ſeated on a throne of Ice, on the pre-
cipitous threſhold of a palace of the ſame material:
the whole ſcene exhibiting a dreary ſpeĉtacle of Rock,
and Ice, and Snow.*

Her throne is guarded by THE GIANTS OF FROST,
*a race of deformed and enormous monſters, whoſe
heads reaching the top of the ſtage, are involved in
clouds and vapours. Their hair and beards formed
of icicles: their Garments of Snow: their complexions
livid, and their forms miſhapen. Meteors play around
their heads ; and ſnow and hailſtones iſſue from their
mouths and noſtrils. A throng of ſhuddering ſpeĉtres
around ; ſome ſauntering about ; others root-bound ;
and all covered with ſnow and icicles. The* DEMONS
OF STORM *and* TEMPEST *wait behind the Chair.*

On the other ſide, in a cave apart, are ſeen THE FATAL
SISTERS *at their Loom. Sculls are fixed to the beams
inſtead of weights ; the chamber is lighted by a Lamp
and a blazing Cauldron.* RAFAEN, *i. e. the Raven
of Schulda hovers over their heads.*

Trio. Urd, Verandi, Schulda.

Weave The Webb—the webb of Fate!
Ply it early—ply it late!
Fates of falling empires weave!
Woes that fuffering mortals grieve!
Spindles turn; the fhuttle throw;
Treacherous joys, and lafting woe,
In the fatal texture grow.
Weave The Woof—the woof of Fate!
Ply it early—ply it late!

Urd. Take the fample from the paft.
Verandi. Prefent forrows thicken faft.
Schulda. But the worft fhall come at laft.
All. Weave The Woof—the woof of Fate!
Ply it early—ply it late!
Fates of falling empires weave!
Woes that fuffering mortals grieve!
Spindles turn—the fhuttle throw.
Treacherous joys and lafting woe
In the fatal texture grow.
Chorus. Weave The Webb—the webb of Fate!
Ply it early—ply it late.

Row. Ceafe, fatal hags! the ill-omen'd yell forego.
Speak: for ye can. I come my fate to know.

Schul. Sorcerefs, yet in early bloom!
Tax us not, but wait thy doom.
Soon enough thy woe fhall come.

Row. Whate'er the will of changeful Fortune be,
I murmur not, nor queftion HER decree.
Weave clofe the fecret woof, ye baleful three.
Not for the gauds of empire now I feek :
Crowns ye may give, and fettled fceptres break.
I fathom not, in this, your dire decree :
For what are crowns and fceptres now to me?
   But of Arthur I muft know—
   Doom of joy ?—or Doom of Woe?

Urd. When firft the fatal bowl you gave,
   And Vortigern became your flave,
   Then for fovran power you pray'd;
   And Fatal Sifters lent their aid.

All. Then for fovran power you pray'd;
   And Fatal Sifters lent their aid.

Row. Sifters thanks : but this I know.

Veran. But now no more ambition fwells:
   Thy fecret foul on Arthur dwells :
   Arthur, who, in Lunvey's groves,
   Ev'n now, in wildering anguifh, roves.

All. Arthur now, in Lunvey's groves,
   In heart-confuming anguifh roves.

Row. Sifters thanks that this I know.
   But yet a further boon beftow.
   Paft and prefent ye have fhown :
   Make, O! make the future known.
   Schulda! fay what you decree ?
   Direfull'ft of the direful three !
   Quick : divine: Is Arthur mine ?
   Schulda! fay what you decree ?

Schul.   Woden fits on Afgard's hills;
      Where Hydraffil's Afh diftills
         Nectar'd drafts of dew divine.
      There alone, in accents clear,
      My Raven whifpers in HIS ear,
         What the future Fates defign.

Row. But I in lore of myftic arts excel,
And Fate's ambiguous book with eafe can fpell.
Speak, Fatal Sifter! fpeak; and I'll explain:
      Tho myftery involve the ftrain.

Sch.   Sifter—ere the memory dye,
      Speak again of things gone by.

Urd.   Once, to fnare a monarch's foul,
      Fair Rowenna drugg'd a bowl.

Row.   I did—I did. Upon my knee,
      Vortigern! I gave it thee.

Sch.   When the bowl again goes round,
      And Vortigern his fleep profound
             Heedlefs quaffs—
          Row. Hela laughs!—
Plain the drift my fenfe defcries.
Sifters thanks.——He dies! he dies!

Hela.   Wide my iron portals throw:
      Perjur'd ghofts defcend below.
      Open throw.   To realms of woe,
      Perjur'd ghofts defcend below.

Row.   Plain the drift my fenfe defcries.
      Hela thanks.——He dies! He dies!

Sch.   Then fhall clofe   Thy jealous woes,

Arthur's hand fhall light the fire
In which thy forrows all expire.

Row. Propitious Schulda! thanks.   But what of her—
The Cambrian viper! hateful Guenever?

Sch.   More thy rival to confound,
Fire and Water fhall furround;
Ruthlefs flames, and waves profound.
Arthur's hand no help fhall lend,
No mortal arm the maid befriend,
Nor aid from pitying Heaven defcend.

Row.   Schulda thanks.   Enough of her
My hated rival Guenever.

Hela.   Wide my iron portals throw:
Perjur'd Ghofts defcend below.
Open—open—open throw!
To realms of woe,
Perjur'd ghofts defcend below.

Row.   Plain the drift my foul defcries.
Vortigern ——He dies!—He dies!
Arthur's hand fhall light the fire
In which my forrows all expire.
Hela's ghofts the joy fhall feel
Joining in the giddy reel!
Lok nor Fenrir fay me nay:
'Tis Rowenna's holyday.

*She waves her wand; and inftantly the whole train of
frozen fpectres rufh to the middle of the ftage, and
join in a fantaftic dance; while all the vocal characters repeat in*

Grand Chorus.

Wide the iron portals throw.
Perjur'd ghofts defcend below.
Hela's fons the triumph feel,
Joining in the giddy reel.—
Lok nor Fenrir fay us nay:
'Tis Rowenna's holiday.

END OF THE FIRST ACT.

ACT. II. SCENE I.

Lynn Savadan: or, Langorfe Pool; by Moonlight.

A Dance of FAIRIES.

1. *Fairy.* While the Moon with filver fheen
　　　　Spangles o'er Savadan's Lake,
　　　Fairies to the margent green
　　　　Hafte from grotto, bower, and brake,
　　　　And in our lunar rites partake.
Chorus. Elves from grotto, bower, and brake,
1. *Fa.*　Frifk it! 2. *Fa.* Frifk it! 3. *Fa.* Frifk it!
Ch.　　Frifk it round the filver lake.
1. *Fa.*　Nor ye who, in your golden boat,
　　　The water-lily, love to float,

Chacing oft, with merry Lay,
The beams that o'er the rippling furface play,
Thefe our lunar rites forfake.
Sem. cho. Elves from grotto, bower, and brake—
Fays that fkim Savadan's lake—
1. *Fa.* Ever gay 2. *Fa.* While ye may.
1. *Fa.* Trip it. 2. *Fa.* Trip it! 3. *Fa.* Trip away!
Cho. Join the dance, and join the lay.
2. *Fa.* Flowers opprest by noontide heat
Let the breath of Fragrance cheer;
And as we brufh with nimble feet,
Blights and Mildews difappear,
And all that taint the vernal year.
Sem. cho. Difappear!—Difappear!—Difappear!—
1. *Fa.* As we whifk it! 2. *Fa.* Frifk it! 3. *Fa.* Whifk it!
1. *Fa.* Whifk it! frifk it! Frifk it! whifk it—
Cho. Let the breath of Fragrance cheer
The vernal year.

The Lady of the Lake *rifes on a Throne of Spars
and Coral, in a car, or water chariot, drawn by
Swans.*

Lady. Enough, ye elves and fairies!—ye who ride
The lunar beam, or on the furface fkim,
Buoyant, of lake or rill, or thro mid air
Beftride the goffamer; and ye who lurk
Beneath my bordering flow'rets, or the leaves
Of penfile fhrubs, that from Savadan's marge
Inhale their frefhnefs.—Well have ye perform'd

Your modeſt functions, from the irriguous haunts,
Chacing the Sterrile Fiend, and all the rout
That hurt with aguiſh ſpells, that neither blight,
Canker, nor ſmut, thro all my favourite bowers,
Infect nor worm appears, of power to mar
The buds of vernal promiſe. 'Tis enough.
Now other cares invite ; and other fears
Swell in my anxious boſom. Arthur's fate
Hangs on the tremulous balance.

From coral groves and ſpar-encruſted dome,
  Where, enthron'd in virgin pride,
  O'er their ſecret urns preſide
   The ſedg'd-crown'd ſiſters fair,
Who make the ſylvan lakes their care,
     I come.
For deep in that ſequeſter'd home
  The voice of Anguiſh pierc'd my ear,
   From Lunvey's echoing groves.
There where hoſtile ſpells ſurrounding
(All his riſing hopes confounding)
  Rack his ſoul with pangs ſevere —
     There — ah ! there —
   Mourning —— pining —
  Every bliſsful thought reſigning —
There bewilder'd Arthur roves.
     For him I grieve,
   For him my coral grots I leave,
Yoke my white ſwans, and breathe this terrene air.

E

Hafte ye Fairies, hafte ye then—
Search the woodland, fearch the glen.
For deeds of love forego your vagrant fport,
And in my fecret grotto make report.

Cho.   Miftrefs, you fhall be obey'd.
1. *Fa.*   Sifters each your province take:
        Mount the breeze, or fkim the lake:
       Thrid with care the leafy fhade.
2. *F.* Frifk it! 3. *F.* Whifk it! 4. *F.* Trip it! 5. *F.* Flit it!
Cho.   Miftrefs you fhall be obey'd.   [*They vanifh.*

The Lady *returns to her Car, and the fcene clofes.*

SCENE II.   *A hanging Wood on the borders of a little Stream.*

Enter Incubus, *fhaking his fingers and rubbing his hands.*

Who-o-o-o! what a poor undone devil am I!   When
I am freezing and dangling on the eves of Hela's palace,
I do nothing but figh and pray that my nechromantic
miftrefs, here, or fome other of my terreftrial employers
would be kind enough to ftand in need of my affiftance,
and give me a blind-man's holiday, in this warmer atmof-
phere; yet here have I been wandering only two or
three hours, and the froft in my joints is converted into
fo horrible a hot-ache, that I begin to wifh my icicle-
fhip had remained undifturbed, in the pure ftate of fub-

terranean congelation, where The Giants of Froſt had
fixed me.   But the worſt is, the night is almoſt ſpent,
and my taſk not completed.   A precious cataplaſm will
be clapped to my ſores, I'll warrant, if I deſcend to
Niflheim again with an imperfect account of my miſſion.

  A plague o'that drunken deſperado, Triſtram! one
by one, I have nabbed all the reſt; and laid the whole
Round Table (knights, ſquires, and all) as quiet as
Mead and Waſſail ever laid them at high feſtival: but
Lok himſelf (the father of all miſchief) cannot get that
dragon-eater out of the reach of Arthur's enchanted
ſword: to hazard the vengeance of which requires a
little more of the fool-valiant than belongs to any devil
of my kidney.—But hold!———A plague on all blun-
derers!   How came I not to think of that before?
What ſort of an angler, for a devil, muſt I be, when a
Welchman was to be caught, not to think of Cwrw?
——Cwrw!! Cwrw!!!——Cwrw!!!!!!——But here
they come.   Bo-peep's the word, and then to my laſt
ſhift.   [Exit.

Enter ARTHUR; and TRISTRAM, *drunk, with a cag.*

Arthur. Diſtraction! furies! whether do we rove?
On what enchanted region have we trod,
Beſet with helliſh fiends?   Mine eyes deceive—
This is not Lunvey.   Theſe are not the groves
Where once, with ſongs prophetic, o'er my head
The miniſtering fairies danc'd, touching my lips
With charm of ſweeteſt numbers, and my limbs

(Yet in their infant fwathes) with iron force
Nerving refiftlefs. Or, if fuch it be,
The Saxon Demons o'er the Ifle prevail,
And our Good Spirits leave us.

Triftram (turning up his cag.) Spirits! O, yes, your
honour's highnefs !—our fpirits are all gone; that's certain.
Here it is, your honour's highnefs! Round and fleek:
—juft the fame big belly it fet out with. But it's delivered your honour's highnefs! fairly delivered; and fo
there's an end to our deliverance.

Hollow! hollow! *(knocking against it with his
knuckles)*—Hollow as a falfe friend, who preaches and
moralifes when Neceffity is at the door: and then he
rings, juft like this—all his fwelling words being nothing
but emptinefs!

Ar. Oh! Guenever! Guenever! At fuch a time!
They could not all defert me. Daftards all!
Chieftains renown'd for hardieft enterprife
Turn daftards on the fpur?——I'll not believe it.

Trift. No, your honour's highnefs! nor little Triftram
neither: any more than he'll believe that his coftrel is a
perpetual fpring; and that it is not, there is heavy proof
in all this lightnefs. *(Throwing it up and catching it.)*
Light! light!—Light as a Courtier's promife—or a Court
Lady's morals.—O that a light coftrel and a dark deftiny
fhould go thus together.—*(As he is toffing the Coftrel
about he tumbles.)* Seated your honour's highnefs!—
Seated!—But what fignifies feating now? The round
table *(placing the cag before him)*—ah! your honour's
highnefs! The round table is quite empty,

Ar. Significant drunkard! doſt thou make a ſcoff
And jeſt of my afflictions?

Triſt. O Lord! your honour's highneſs! quite the
contrary. Moraliſing, your honour—moraliſing. Inſpi-
red!—ſpiritualiſed!—What were good liquor good for,
if it did not put good thoughts into one's head?

Ar. It is enchantment all. Demoniac ſpells
Have ſnar'd their feet, and Hell's ſuborned fiends
Have with inceſtuous Vortigern conſpir'd
To mock my high-rais'd hopes. Oh! ſacred wax!
(pulling out a pair of Tablets and preſſing them to his lips)
Grav'd with the ſweeteſt words, by faireſt hands —
And yet how terrible!——Dear, direful proof
Of chaſteſt conſtancy!——This night—this night—
With ſuch a cauſe to charm them to their oaths
Could they have fled, like rècreants?

Triſt. Fl-e-ed! O yes, your honour's highneſs; flown,
I'll anſwer for them: but it was at ſecond hand; as they
trot when they ride o' cockhorſe. I'll ſwear by a full
coſtrel—(for it would be but an empty oath to ſwear by
a coſtrel that was not full—and would ſhew me, as it
were, to be but a 'ſquire of hollow faith) I ſaw the
Devil fly away with half a dozen of them. I ſup-
poſe if it had not been for my Guardian Spirit *(lifting
up the cag)* I ſhould have known myſelf what ſort of a
poney His Devilſhip is. And then—ha! ha! ha! ha!

Ar. Peace, babbling Jeſter! Art thou too poſſeſt?

Triſt. Ho! ho! ho! I beg pardon, your honour's
highneſs—but i'faith I can't help laughing, to think—
ha! ha! ha! if the Devil had laid hold of me, what a

figure I fhould have made, charioteering between a pair
of footy wings, with two great horns in my hands, by
way of reins, and a huge pair of faucer eyes before me,
for lanthorns.—Ho! ho! ho!—What a dafh!

 Ar. (ftill grafping The Tablets, *and gazing upon them*
  with encreafed emotion.) This night—this night—
The laft permitted to the anxious calm
Of Innocence unviolate!—This Night
That, midft the curtain'd filence, ftill fhall talk
Of its fucceffor's horrors—of the hour
When the foul father lover (fo decreed)
Flufh'd from the riotous banquet—luft enflam'd!—
Inebriate to inceft!————Hell is there!—

 He walks, diftraEtedly feveral times, to and fro; then
  paufes—opens the tablets again, and reads.
 " This night, this night!—all means of death remov'd,
 " (The laft poor refpite tears and prayers could gain)
 " I give to thoughts of Thee, and to thofe vows
 " Of chafteft love inviolate we pledg'd
 " On Ufk's remember'd banks. This night (yet pure)
 " I dare to think I am Arthur's. All beyond—
 " All if Gwrtheyrnion's walls————But hafte and fave!
 " Hafte with thy Warrior Knights—Oh! that this breath,
 " That never flows but to wing prayers to Heaven
 " For thee and for thy fafety—that this breath ————
 " But worfe impends—Worfe to *thy* heart—to *mine!*
 " —To mine!—Oh! perfecuting Heaven! that aught
 " Than Arthur's fafety—Arthur's facred life
 " Can be more precious to the fhuddering heart
 " Of his difaftrous Guenever!"

Defpair !————

" But hafte and fave ! Hafte with thy warrior knights !"
Alas ! where are they ? Ho ! ye recreants, ho !————

Follow me.   Once again, with hopelefs fearch,
Thro the night-thickened labyrinths let us wind,
Wakening the fullen Echoes ; if perforce,
With their reverberate aid, our fhouts may reach
The chance-bewilder'd ftraglers———if but Chance,
Not Hell, or fouler Treachery, have fapt
Their faith till now undoubted.——Ho ! what ho !

My Guenever !—difaftrous Guenever !   [*Exit.*

Trift. Oh ! my Coftrel !———my fweet, lovely——
poor, miferable, empty Coftrel !

Aye—There's the Devil ! But for that, the adventure would not yet be defperate.   There would ftill be
three of us—the redoubtable Triftram, the puiffant Arthur, and the all-conquering Cwrw : and what could ftand
before us ?—Caer Gwrtheyrnion ?—Pho !—nor all the
Cares in the univerfe.   Why we fhould'n't care for Pan-
demonium itfelf.   We'd ftorm old Belzebub in his
grand keep ; and make a rareefhow of all his family.

Send us, ye Guardian Angels ! fend us but a coftrel
of Cwrw ! of C—W—R—W. Fal de rol de rol, de ra ra,
lol lol !   *(Sings.)*

A large cafk rifes out of the ground, againft which
Tristram runs his nofe as he is reeling out.

Bawh ! What have we here ? Ho ! ho ! a cafk ! a
cafk.—The prayers of the drunken fhall be heard ; for
they pray in The Spirit. But what is this ?—Some magical
infcription I fuppofe.   O thou univerfal lamplightrefs,—

thou that fee'ft many a thing that thy elder brother, the
Sun, never dreamt of!—lend me thy fpectacles awhile,
that I may fpell. C—W—R—W—Cwrw!!—Spell,
indeed—What are your Runic Rhymes, your Riddles,
your Pharmaceutrias—your Cabals, your Abracadaberas,
to the magical combination of C—W—R—W? *(Sings.*

> Of fpells you may talk,
>   Writ in ink, blood, or chalk,
> With which Wizzard and Witch have to do;
>   But each Welchman can tell
>   That there never was fpell
> Like C—W—R—W!   Fal de rol. &c.

> With this fpell, I'll be bound
>   To make Nature fpin round,
> As our boys with their whip-tops can do;
>   And the world all fo fcurvy
>   I'd turn topfyturvy
> With C—W—R—W.   Fal de rol! &c.

Infpir'd—Infpir'd! If it be but as potent to valour as
to verfe, the bufinefs is done.—And where's the doubt?
What but Cwrw was it, that produced fo many famous
heroes of antiquity, from Nimrod to Jack the Giant
Killer.   *(Sings.)*

> O, ye heroes renown'd
>   Who fought all the world round—
> O! ye Cæfars, and fam'd Alexanders!

Pray how had ye thriv'd,
If of Cwrw depriv'd?
Faith you'ad been juſt as valiant as ganders.

      Fal de rol! &c.

If a ſecond you want,
Then, each foeman to daunt,
Then, I'll tell you, my boy, what to do;
Never fear to depend
On the Welchman's beſt friend,
On C—W—R—W. Fal de rol! &c.

Bravo! bravo, little Triſtram! One draught of this genuine water of the muſes, and thou wilt eclipſe all the Knights of the Round Table, and bear away the prize, in the bardic circles, from Talieſſin himſelf. But how to get at it? Oh! A ſpile!—A ſpile!—I'll anſwer for it then it ſhall not be ſpoiled. *(Pulls out the ſpile, and the ale begins to run.)* Genuine! genuine! entire! I'll be ſworn. A choice drop out of the celeſtial cellar, brewed by my Guardian Angel for his own private drinking. Let me take it devoutly. *(Kneeling)* Now, now ſhall I be famous, or the devil is in it. *(Drinks. The head of the Caſk flies off, out of which* INCUBUS *riſes, and ſeizes him by the ears.)*

Inc. Aye, and in it he is: little as you might expeƈt it. *(The caſk ſinks down and leaves* TRISTRAM *in the clutches of* INCUBUS.*)*

Triſt. (Shivering.) Who-o-o-who are you, and be-e hanged to you?

Inc. A devil!

F

Trift. The-e-e devil you are. Wha-a-at the devil makes my teeth chatter fo then? In fuch hands, I fhould have expected to be frying in my own greafe.

Inc. Aye, that's becaufe you don't know what fort of devil you have to deal with, my little Triftram. I am none of your bon-fire devils come to entertain you with fquibs and crackers, and birth-day rockets and illuminations: but a good thorough icicle devil, from the regions of Hela: where I have been freezing, under the North Pole, for more than half a century.

Trift. Fre-e-e-ezing with a ve-e-e-engeance! Zounds I am fro-o-o-o-ozen too. I-i-i-i-— can't get to my fw-o-o-o-ord.

          Ar-r-r r-Arthur!

Inc.   Vainly you for Arthur call:
       Your very words are frozen all:
         They fhall never reach his ear.

Trift.   Ar-r-r r Arthur! Arthur! co-o-o-ome away.
      I am lo-o o-o-loft if yo-u-u-u delay.

Inc.   Truft me he fhall never hear.
        Your words are frozen.

Trift.   So-o-o-o I————fear.

Inc.   Thus upon my prey I feize.

Trift.   I freeze—I freeze—I fre-e-eze!
         Ar-r-r Arthur!—Ar-r-r Arthur.

Inc.   'Tis in vain   Your lungs you ftrain.

Trift.   I-i-i-i—I fee it plain.

Inc.   Vaffal hind!   Your voice I bind—

Trift.   S o o-o-o I find—

Inc.   In Vindfualer's icy chain'

Trift.   W-w-w-w-wind! wind fwallow!
                        Cold and hollow!

Inc.   Grim Vindfualer! Winter's fire!

Trift. Ar-r-r-r Arthur! Arthur! O-o-o-oh! a fire!

Inc.   'Tis in vain; Fruitlefs pain; Thus to ftrain.
           Arthur, Arthur cannot hear.

Trift. So-o-o-o-o I fear.   *Inc.* It is clear.
          So, little Triftram? come you here.
                My potent miftrefs thus to pleafe,
                Upon my fhivering prey I feize.

Trift.   I fre - e - e - e - e - e - e - e - eze!

Cho. of Knights without. We fre - e - e - e - e - e - eze!

> Tristram *finks down in a ftate of torpor; over-*
> *powered by the benumbing influence of the Demon;*
> *and* Incubus *drags him off the ftage.*

Re-enter Arthur.

Triftram! Triftram!—Art thou alfo gone?
Vanifh'd thro air? or fwallow'd by the earth?
The laft of all my hoft!   Infernal fiends!
Are there no means to reach ye? Out good fword!
Whofe tenfold temper, fteep'd in myftic dews
By the fair regent of Savadan's lake,
No goblin fpell refifts.   On flocks and ftones,
And each ambiguous thing my eyes fhall meet,
I'll try its force.   If chance fome lurking fiend
Start up reveal'd; ere now this arm, unftaid,
Hath tam'd fuch foes, and to their hoftile hell
Difmifs'd them howling.   Nerve it now, ye powers

Who fmile on virgin innocence. .I ftrike
In Nature's caufe; for love and Guenever! [*Exit.*

SCENE III. *Enter Fairies.*

1. *Fa.* Sifters! Sifters!   2. *Fa.* Whift ye! Whift!

1. *Fa.* Tell me — tell me what ye lift.

3. *Fa.* Things of moment hover nigh.

1. *Fa.* Who can read them.   2 *Fa.* I.   3 *Fa.* And I.

Cho.   Things of moment hover nigh.

1. *Fa.* Sifters! Sifters!   2. *Fa.* Lift ye! Lift!

3. *Fa.* Tell me fairies what ye wift?

1. *Fa.* Tell me what ye read on high?

2. *Fa.* Fading flars, 3. *Fa.* And morning nigh.

1. *Fa.* Who can fee it? 2. *Fa.* I.   3. *Fa.* And I.

Cho. . To the Grotto—hafte away.

4. *Fa.* You have feen it? 1. *F.* Aye! 2. *F.* Aye! 3. *F.* Aye!

Cho.   To the Grotto whifp away.

1. *Fa.* Frifk it!   2. *Fa.* Whifk it!

3. *Fa.* Trip it! 1. *F.* Whip it.

4. *Fa.* To the Grotto—flit away!

Cho. What we've witnefs'd there difplay.   [*Exeunt.*

SCENE IV. *The Lake, feen in a new afpect.* ·*The Sun rifing above the neighbouring mountains.*

Enter ROWENNA [*attended.*]

The fhades of night difperfe, and o'er the hills
(The Eaftern bound of Cambria) Balder's fteed
Rufhes with reinlefs neck, and to the winds

Gives his bright mane of orient, ſtreaming far
Thro the illumin'd ſky.   The dazzling ray,
With tint reflective, over ſtream and lake,
Plays with the morning breeze; and leaf and flow'r,
Moiſt with the tears of evening, bend ſurcharg'd
With mimic radiance : every cryſtal ſphere
Pencil'd with rays minute — as tho inſtinct,
Each with its fairy ſun — a fairy world.
'Tis ſplendour all, and gladneſs — All but here,
Where one lov'd object, filling every thought,
Blots out Creation.   Sound nor ſight can pleaſe,
But what relates to Arthur : and this hope
Of quick poſſeſſion, from the Fatal maids,
With poignant expectation but enflames
The frenzy it ſhould ſooth.

     In vain empaſſion'd Hope I feed
        With promis'd boons of hovering joy :
     The expected bliſs, by Fate decreed,
        Doubts and chilling fears annoy.

     In vain the empaſſion'd heart to eaſe,
        The ſplendid ſcenes of morn I trace :
     Whate'er the raptur'd eye ſhould pleaſe,
        Doubts and chilling fears deface.

     Diſtracting doubts, and chilling fears
        What touch of ſenſe can charm away ?
     A blank the ſmiling dawn appears :
        And mute to me the vernal lay.

Propitious Goddefs! hear my pray'r!
Nor long the promis'd blifs delay :
The fmiling morn fhall then be fair,
And Rapture tune-the vernal lay.

Near to this fpot, among the bordering woods —
So fung the Fatal Sifters (and the fong
But now the oafifh Incubus confirm'd)
My Arthur roves, now ifolate. O guide
His fteps, benignant Frea! that mine eyes
May gaze to fulnefs, and my pleaded love
Effay his fecret heart. 'Tis heard. He comes :
With what a tempeft gathering on his brow!
Yet lovely in his anger. We'll obferve
A while, unnoted, till the ftorm is fpent :
Then, o'er the waves fubfiding, Love fhall fmile ;
And woo The Bird of Peace.   [*They retire*

Enter ARTHUR.

   Arth. 'Tis fruitlefs fearch —
I toil myfelf in vain. Enchantment here
Dwells not — or dwells beyond the boafted reach
Of gifted countercharm.   And, lo! the Sun,
Climbing his fouthering arch, with gilded fmile,
Mocks at my bootlefs rage ; while grove and vale,
Mountain, and headlong ftream, and placid lake
Shine in the record of my baffled hopes,
My fhame, and my diftraction.
            Row. Queen of fmiles !
Who blend'ft confenting hearts in mutual blifs,

Be it my talk to footh him.

     Arth. Ye twin heights
Of bleak Farinioch!—Ye whofe alpine heads
Catch the firft rays of Morning! I had hopes,
Ere down your floping fides encroaching light
Had chac'd the lingering fhadows, o'er your brow
(Girt with my warrior knights in firm array)
To have pour'd the fhout of battle; on the walls
Of doom'd Gwrtheyrnion, like the vollying cloud,
To have burft in direful thunders; broke the chains
Of Saxon ufurpation; from the rape
Of threaten'd inceft fnatch'd the weeping maid,
And hung the wreaths of Love on Glory's fane.

  Row. Empire, and Love, and Glory! Frea, hear—
Make them the three-fold dower, " When Authur's hand
" Shall light the flame in which my woes expire!"

 I feel confenting Heav'n. Some whifper'd voice
Tells me the prayer is heard :—perchance the maid
Whom frequent The Propitious Goddefs fends
To cheer the love-lorn votary. *(She comes forward.)*
     Arthur, hail!
One not to Grief unknown your grief's would heal.

 Arth. *(wrapt in foliloquy, and not obferving her.)*
Sweet bud of virgin innocence! fhall HE,
The inceftuous father, blaft thy opening charms,
And rifle thy pure fragrance? while mine arm
(Awful in foreign confliĉt) here, at home,
Sinks palfied, and, in Love's,—in Nature's caufe,
Hangs powerlefs by my fide!——O Guenever!
Soul of my foul!—Oh charms, above all charm!

Trancendant in their lovelinefs ! once deem'd
My fole fequefter'd treafure !—Paradife
Of all my thoughts ! and of my nightly dreams
Sole vifitant—when, pure as winnow'd fnows,
That from the peaky Vans, till fpring matures,
Gleam on the dazzled traveller, thou cam'ft,
With funny fmiles of fanctity and love,
Bleffing my pillow'd flumber.—Guenever !
Hope's vital fountain !—

        Row. (afide)   Progeny of Lok !
Does Fenrir howl this difcord in mine ear ?
Or charnel Grymer bark ?—What founds are thefe ?
Where is thy promife, Frea ?—Schulda, where
Thy hopes oracular ?

        Arth. Oh ! Sweet of Sweets !
Perfonified perfection !—tint ! and form !
And types of inward excellence ! that fhines
Thro the tranfparent veil.   Eyes ! lips ! and cheeks
Vermeil'd with angel modefty ! and fwell
Of foft ingenuous bofom, yet unfunn'd
By Love's prefumptuous gaze !—all Vortigerns ?—
Inceftuous Vortigerns !

        Row. Can I bear this ?
Furies of Hela's fhades ! Ye Fiends of Storm !
What are your tempefts to the tempeft here ?
Are thefe my hopes ? Down, down, my ftruggling foul,
And truft The Fates.   Be calm ; or thou art loft.

                     [She retires.
    Arth. With what a lengthen'd ftride the luftful Sun
Haftens the hour of horrors ; towards the couch

Of weſtern Thetis ſtraining, ere as yet
The bluſh of parting from her orient cheek
The winnowing winds have bruſh'd.
　　　　　　　Check, check thy ſpeed!
Reſtrain thy bridegroom haſte: awhile forego
The fiery track, 'till pitying heav'n afford
Means of preventive vengeance: from the clouds
That curtain thy repoſe, leſt Heſper thruſt
His guilty lamp, to mark the fated hour,
And light the tyrant Vortigern to deeds
That make Hell tremble.

ROWENNA *(re-entering, with* EDELTHRED, *at a
　　　diſtance.)* Paſſion ſhakes him ſtill:
But I am calm, in confidence renew'd,
And wait predicted bliſs.
　　　　　　Arth. My pray'rs are vain.
I war with woman's weapons: fall'n—reduc'd
To woman's impotence: with ſenſeleſs brawl
Diſturbing the calm elements, that laugh
My rage to ſcorn.　Come then, thou ſullen Calm
Of conſcious deſperation, thro my ſoul
Breathe thy narcotic influence—ſteep each nerve
In opiate dews, and o'er each maddening ſenſe,
Bewilder'd, from their chilling urns pour forth
Thy inaneſcent torpors, till no more
Reflection wakes, and dull Oblivion drop
The vail by Fancy lifted.
　　　　　　Row. (aſide.) Be it ſo,
Benignant Frea! then to other ſcenes,

G

Joyous, awake reviving Confcioufnefs,
Made happy in the change !

    Arthur. Hear, hear them not—
Hear not the fhrieks, my foul, that, thro the gloom,
Rending Gwrtheyrnion's towers, with vain appeal,
Call on the name of Arthur.—Reft thou here,
My wearied foul—reft here ; even on this oak,
Which, ere matur'd, the lightning's fork hath fcath'd,
Or Whirlwind's arm lopt brief :—here fit and mufe
In moralifing vacancy, abridg'd
Of vital virtue ; like this faplefs trunk,
To lift no more the flourifhing head to heaven,
Or fpread the arms of fhelter.

    Row. Edelthred,
The ftorm is paft.—Lift how to murmurs foft,
And wailings inarticulate, fubfides
The roaring furge of paffion. Shall I fpeak ;
Or wait the heavings of thefe waves, that yet
Would lafh themfelves to ftilnefs ?

    Arth. You, ye Pomps
Of unavailing war—fire-plumed helm,
And burnifh'd fhield emblazon'd ; and thou gift
Of her my fometime guardian, lie ye there,
Till the flow ruft confumes ; or o'er your fame
The monumental weed, with unfhorn head,
Bends vailing : for no more fhall Arthur's arm,
That fail'd to refcue Guenever, defcend
On dint of meaner argument to try
Your charmed temper.

He throws away his helmet, his shield, and his en-
chanted sword; and, seating himself in a disconsolate
attitude, upon the shattered Oak, continues to pore upon
the ground, in vacant agony.

     Row.   Past my best hopes !—
Propitious Frea ! now the webb untwines
Spun by The Destinies.   The magic sword
Falls from his grasp, unconscious :—now no more
From power of Runic verse, or magic spell,
Or from Rowenna's charmed wand exempt.

  My Fates prevail. Agga ! my rod—my rod !

[*Enter* AGGA, *with the wand.* ROWENNA *waves it*
  over the head of ARTHUR; *and* HE *sleeps.*]

Sleep on his troubled lids awhile descend,
Till we the charm of Runic numbers end.

    Evles who shun the chilly moon !
    Demons of the sultry noon !
Response ⎱ Whose the voice that now ascends
of spirits ⎰ The abodes of Alfheim ?
Edel.   Hers who rends
    With spells the pitchy vail of Night—
Agg.   And blots the settled orbs of light.
Row.   Demons of the sultry noon !
     My call attend.
Resp.   Soon we greet thee—mistress, soon.
Row.   But not in gorgon pomp descend.

Edel.   Far hence, ye haggard forms of Fear!
        Horror, vail'd in mirky brow,
     Rage, that fcorns the Pitying tear,
        Griefs, that low to Hertha bow.
     Other forms than thefe muft move
        Soft confent,   Sweet content—
     Soft confent and mutual love!

Refp.   Other forms than thefe fhall move
     Soft confent and mutual love,

Agg.   Hafte in dimpled fmiles array'd
        Such as fport in Frea's train,
     When fhe tempts the blufhing maid,
        Half afraid,   To the fhade,
     Sighing, dying, where the fwain
     Fears the promis'd blifs delay'd.

Refp.   Such the fmiling forms that move
     Soft confent, and mutual love.

Row.   Thus, to weave the myftic chain,
        Demons of the Noon repair:
     But to vulgar eyes remain
        Viewlefs as impaffive air.

A troop of DEMONS *rufh on the ftage, in the femblance
of winged boys, crowned with wreaths of flowers, and
arrayed in effeminate apparel.—Strings of rofes in
their hands; with which they link themfelves together,
in intricate circles, and dance round* ARTHUR, *as
he fleeps. Others play with his armour, and one, of fupe-
rior fize and appearance, takes poffeffion of his fword.*

Row. The charm of Runic numbers now complete—
From Arthur's eyes ye drowfy fumes retreat.
Awake to Joy—for every joy is here
To charm the eye and footh the liftening ear.

Cho.   Joy fincere   Hovers near;
          Wake to fee; and wake to hear.

Arth. What antic troop are ye, whofe mid-day dreams
Difturb a wretch's flumbers? Hence! Avaunt!

*He endeavours to difentangle himfelf. They encircle him
with their fillets, &c. Singing the following Glee.*

          Doughty hero! lay afide
          Sullen looks and martial pride:
            Love and Pleafure wait you here.
              Love and Pleafure,
              Without meafure,
              Ope their treafure:
            Melting Love, and Joy fincere!
Cho.   Love and Pleafure revel here.

Arth.   My Sword! My Sword!

*They laugh and dance round him; twining their fillets
clofer and clofer: and repeating, in chorus.*

          Doughty hero! lay afide
          Sullen looks and martial pride:
            Love and Pleafure revel here,

Arth. Diftraction! Infamy! infnar'd! inthrall'd!
Bound in a fillet, like fome harlot's toy!

This—only this, was wanting to complete
My fum of wretchednefs.

           Row. Of rapture fay :
For fuch I come to offer. Generous Arthur!
Too long by an unworthy flame inthrall'd
To an inceftuous wanton : lo! my Charm
Shall fet you free: and on a worthier choice
Empire and Love await, and deathlefs Fame.

In the bofom of youth fay what wifhes can glow
That my power cannot grant, or my favour beftow ?
Thefe beauties that monarchs have ftruggled to gain,
I offer unafk'd.——Shall I offer in vain ?
No ; heart with heart meeting, and clafp'd in thefe arms,
Your bofom fhall throb to foft paffion's alarms.
         Heart to heart fondly beating !
         Our vows ftill repeating !
Reclining!   Refigning   To paffions alarms—
Our bofoms ftill throbbing !—enfolding our arms !

Then the fceptre of Britain, by Schulda decreed
To await on my love, I prefent as thy meed.
Thefe beauties that monarchs have ftruggled to gain,
I offer thus dower'd.—Can I offer in vain ?
While thus, with heart meeting, I ftretch forth my arms,
Ambition and Beauty uniting their charms,
         Can your heart coldly beating,
         From Rapture retreating,
Difdaining!   ! Refraining   From paffions alarms,
An Empire relinquifh, and fly from thefe arms?

Then my magic fhall aid, and my verfe fhall record
All the deathlefs exploits of your lanee, and your fword;
And the glory that heroes have ftruggled to gain
I offer fecure.—Shall I offer in vain?
No; heart to heart beating, and clafp'd in thefe arms
Love, Glory, and Empire fhall mingle their charms.
   Heart to heart fondly beating!
   Our vows ftill repeating!
Reclining! Refigning To paffions alarms
Our bofoms ftill throbbing!—enfolding our arms!

Arth. Sorcerefs of Elb! devoted Britain's curfe!
Hence with thy wanton chant. Tho thus inthrall'd—
Betray'd by Love's affliction (fentient there
Beyond a maiden's fofinefs) in thefe bonds
Powerlefs I ftand, yet can my foul difdain
Thy blandifh'd witcheries. A Crown from thee?
Love, Glory, and Ambition! Are they things
Of fuch abhor'd conjunction as to blend
With thy pollutions?—I'd abjure them, then—
Flee to fome hermit's cave—unfex myfelf,
And, in the mirkieft mine, drudge out, in toil
Obfcene, and fervile bonds, the dregs of life
Difhonour'd. For the World to Chaos runs—
The bleffed Sun no more his luftrous beam
Sheds on created order, if fuch gifts
Depend upon fuch givers.
     Row. Down my heart!—
Injurious Arthur! even this from thee,
Rowenna's love can pardon.

Arth. Love !—Thy Love ?
The love of Vortigern's polluted wife ?

Row. The love of her who was, erewhile, the wife
Of the polluted Vortigern. · But crimes
Like his diffolve the fettled charities
Of conjugal affiance.

Arth. O ! no doubt
With Purity like thine.   And he who (urg'd
By lures, by incantations, and the bowl
Spic'd with lafcivious philters) made thee room
For royal fpoufals in a murderer's bed—
He who, feduc'd by thy idolatrous faith,
Forgot the chafte affinities that link
The focial frame of Nature—

Row. ——Speak—Speak out.
Why does thy ftruggling foul forbear to name
What yet it dwells on moft ?—He whofe vile luft
Makes wanton revel in a daughter's arms—
(The arms of Guenever !) deferves to pay
The deftin'd forfeit of his crime, and hers.

Arth. His crime and Hers ! Makes wanton revel ! Hers?
He has not fure————

Row. No fure. The diligent fpeed
With which fhe fcap'd his cuftody, what time
(Dreadful in Saxon flaughter) you purfu'd
This father lover headlong thwart the realm,
Proves with what fix'd abhorrence fhe regards
His lawlefs love, and how prepar'd fhe ftands
To ACT the virgin coynefs fhe profeffes.

Arth. Diftraction ! Furies !

           Row. What if now my art
Should ſtretch thy viſion thro intruding ſpace —
Rendering the opaque of matter to thy ſight
Pervious and clear (for ſo by ſpells I can,)
And ſhew thee thy deluſion—ſhew, reveal'd,
Their preſent aƈt! and in what amorous folds
They wanton, ſhamelefs?
           Arth. Give me firſt my ſword;
Touch'd by whoſe virtue each deluſive birth
Of magic dies—abortive: elſe thy ſpell,
Mocking the couzen'd ſenſes, might betray,
And damn me with illuſion. Eaſier far
To clothe ſome air-drawn phantom in the form
Of her thy hate calumniates, than to pierce
With ſtretch of human ken (however ſharpen'd)
Yon mountain's, peaky maſs, that bars the ſight
Towards Gwrtheyrnion.
           Sorcerefs! doſt thou blench
The late-fluſh'd cheek, and, with abated eye,
Admit deteƈtion?   Yes; thou ſtand'ſt reveal'd.
   Henceforth thy arts at lower quarry fly;
Nor think to taint, with nechromantic frauds,
The fame of Guenever, whoſe virtue towers,
(Tranſcendent, like her beauty) far above
Thy foul contaminations: like the orb
That rules the tranquil night—luſtrous and pure !—
That on the wolfiſh howl of Calumny
Smiles, and ſhines on, unalter'd.
           Row. Death to ᵖᵖe !
This conſtancy appals me: and my foul

Scarce in The Fatal Sisters more confides,
Or Frea's whisper'd promise.   Yet remains
One only effort.   Bind him fast, ye elves,
With your enchanted braids.   His eyes shall see
Within Gwrtheyrnion's walls—his ears shall hear
What distant he regards not.

     Yes, by Hela!   *(aside.)*
Charm-bound from voice or motion, he shall view
The consummated rape; and his sick soul,
Loathing what now he dotes on, shall resign
To her predestin'd fate this hated she—
This vaunted Paragon.   Then, Vortigern,
Thy Cup awaits thee; and my Arthur's hand
Shall light the flame in which my woes expire.

     My Fate is in my hand.
   I feel my kindling passions move,
    Great with Vengeance, great with Love!
Prophetic scenes of promis'd rapture rise;
    Doubts disperse, and hopes expand.
   Away with suppliant sighs!
   Hope returns: Dejection flies:
   I feel the kindling passions rise:
     My Fate is in my hand.

As they are binding ARTHUR, *a symphony of soft music is heard from the Lake.* THE LADY *rises in her
Car.* THE DEMONS *drop the sword, &c. in great
consternation; and dispersing, are seen flying thro the
air, in their proper appearances of deformity; with a*

confufed and fearful clamour. ROWENNA *and her Attendants run out on the oppofite fide.*

Lady. Goblins avaunt ! nor impious, thus profane
My fylvan confines and irriguous reign.
   And thou, brave Prince ! behold again reftor'd
Thy ravifh'd freedom, and thy magic fword :
For, not forgetful of my former love,
Your griefs afflict me, and your dangers move.
Your weak defpair yourfelf will freely blame :
Go,—force your pardon in the field of fame.
Your Knights and Squires already marfhall'd ftand,
By me redeem'd, and wait for your command.
Refrefh'd and vigorous from the genial right,
They burn impatient, and demand the fight ;
Not far remote from yon embowering fcreen.
My inftant power fhall waft you to the fcene.

*SCENE V. She waves her trident ; and the fcene inftant-
ly changes to a thicket at the foot of The Beacons.*

THE KNIGHTS OF THE ROUND TABLE *appear as
juft rifing from their repaft.*—TALIESSIN *and other*
BARDS—*playing on their harps. Horfes ranged on
each fide of the ftage, and the 'Squires holding them.*
——*Flourifh.*
As the KNIGHTS *perceive* ARTHUR, *they flock
around him ; and* TALIESSIN *fings the following
Air*—

Arthur comes, to Britain dear :
    Bid the brazen trumpets blow.
Led by him, we cannot fear
    Civil rage or foreign foe.

Chorus *of Bards and Knights.*

Arthur hail ! to Britain dear :
    Loud ye brazen trumpets blow.
Led by Thee, we cannot fear
    Civil rage, or foreign foe.   [*Flourish.*

Arth. No thanks, my gallant comrades ! 'Tis no time
For verbiage now.   We'll write our courtesies
Deep on the foemen's backs. Gwrtheyrnion falls.
My sword is out.   The word is—Guenever.
            [*They draw. Flourish.*

Tal.   Let the streaming banner fly.
        Wave your flaming falchions high.
        Guenever, and Victory !

Cho.   See the streaming banner fly.
        See our falchions flaming high.
        Guenever, and Victory !

Lady. Go, friends of Virtue, Honour, Justice, Love !
Confirm your Glory, and your worth approve.
To higher powers I now resign my care,
Then seek my sparry Grot and coral Chair.

Thee—fire-eye'd Seraph!—thee,
That, on thy faphir throne,
Among The Spheres,
With ever-wakeful miniftry,
Brac'd in adamantine zone,
Mak'ft fea-girt Albion's caufe thy own—
Thee, whom the Warrior Hoft reveres!
Thee, whom the bleeding Battle fears!
On thee I call.
As oft thy guardian care hath fpread
The fhield of fafety o'er the Patriot's head,
Bidding the iron tempeft vainly fall,
Propitious now on Arthur fmile,
And guard the warrior boaft of Britain's ifle
From Foes uplifted mace, and Treafon's fecret thrall.
Cho.   Thee! whom the warrior hoft reveres—
Thee! whom the bleeding Battle fears—
On thee we call!

Tal.   Spread the fervour—fpread the fong,
Spread the martial flame along,
Rufh to fight with loud acclaim;
Warm'd by that Seraphic Power
Who, high-enthron'd in empyrean bower,
Watchful for Albion, joys to wield
The fword of flame;
And the adamantine fhield,
Amid'ft the direful conflict, fpreads
O'er the confecrated heads
Of chiefs devote to patriot fame.

Chorus. Spread the fervour—fpread the fong—
  Spread the martial flame along.

Ar. Sound drums and trumpets.—Bid the martial fife
Pierce the charm'd ear of Valour. Sound the charge.
The caufe is Freedom, Love, and Guenever!

Chorus. Wave the falchion—couch the fpear—
  Blow the brazen trumpet, blow.—
  Arthur leads: we cannot fear
  Civil rage, or foreign foe.

The Lady of the Lake *defcends, while* the Knights *march acrofs the ftage in order of attack, amidft a flourifh of martial inftruments.*

END OF THE SECOND ACT.

ACT. III. SCENE I.

The infide of the Caftle Gwrtheyrnion. Several fervants crofs the ftage; bearing boughs and ftrings of flowers, difhes, Goblets, &c. as in preparation for a fumptuous banquet.

 Enter Tristram *and* Scout.

 Trift. Well, here we are, Scout, found wind and limb, within the Caftle. Our adventure begins under moft happy aufpices. Our tale of defertion paffes mufter, without fufpicion.   Our proffered affiftance feems to be very acceptable : and thefe preparations betoken no meagre reception.   One would think we had followed the heel of Victory, rather than trod on the toe of approaching Action.

Scout. Toe ! brother Triftram ! why 'tis the very corn we have trod on, to tell my mind o' the matter. Would we were well thro with it.   It is a project big with dangers.

Trift. Big with water, like a dropfy, you well-hunter ! You fwill your coward Fears with the draught of Temperance, as you call it, till every kilderkin of apprehenfion becomes a butt ; while I, with more inebriate wifdom, never fee dangers, but by reflection, on the outfide of a goblet, or at the bottom of a well polifhed tankard ; where the convexity of the medium diminifhes their proportions and fhrinks them into infignificance.

But away to your tafk.   There is no time to lofe. And as Providence has bleft thee with a fine lying face of thy own, honour thy creator by making the moft of it.

Scout. Never fear me.   Remember but your own part as ftoutly.

Trift. Mine. Pho ! my memory is on the edge of my fword :—keen and durable. Do you but lie and wriggle and intrigue through the firft part of the bufinefs—if I do not fight thro the other, may I never be drunk again with the 'Squires of the Round Table. So away to your quirks and your quibbles, and contrive to give the princefs Guenever an item of what is in agitation. Remember—the lone tower is the place. You will find

my Sword and me at the draw bridge, at the time ap-
pointed.　　　　　　　　　　　　[*Exit* SCOUT.

In the mean time, as I am no dab at intrigue, I will
endeavour to kill time, till the time of killing arrives,
with fome fool's fport among thefe fcullions.　[*Exit.*

SCENE II.　*The Servants, &c. ftill continue croffing
the Stage.*

Enter ROWENNA, *mufing.*

　　" When the bowl again goes round,
　　" And Vortigern his fleep profound
　　　　　　" Heedlefs quaffs!"———
O! impotence of memory! to o'erlook
The fated fign, and, with diforder'd fpeed,
Anticipate my deftinies!　　For this
My Gods forfake me: to the adverfe power
Of dull Savadan's elfin regent elfe
Not obvious.　But with happier omens now,
And preordain'd progreffion, I advance
The twofold work of Fate.　　Why aye—proceed
Ye menial herd—Mechanic inftruments—
Unconfcious pivots in the ftate machine
With which the powerful work!—prepare the feaft—
Drefs up the joyous hall, with boughs, and braids
Of flaunting fragrance—hung be every feat
With fweets coronal; and the banquet heap
To feign'd Conciliation: nor fufpeɛt
What Fate and I determine.　Vortigern!

Now feed thy foul voluptuous. Hafte—prepare
To revel out thy laft : for, even now,
The bowl is pregnant ; and the ambrofial draught
Teems with thy fate matur'd. Soon—foon he quaffs—
Quaffs his laft fleep profound. Then comes the crown
Of all my feverifh hopes ; and Arthur's hand
Lights up the flame in which my woes expire.

 But, lo ! the Banquet waits. I go to greet
At once the nuptial, and funereal treat.
Yet, ere on Frea's name I dare to call,
Defcend ye handmaids of the fhield-roof'd hall.

  Sifters three, in fearful ftate,
  Who at Valhalla's banquet wait,
    Watching the nod
 Of him, fupreme, The Warrior God,
  Who, midft the genial rite,
While blithe the amber goblet circles round,
  Thro you, inflicts the deftin'd wound,
   And thins the ranks of fight !——
 On you, who wait by Woden's fide,
 (The daftard's dread, the warrior's pride)
    I call—
 To hover round Gwrtheyrnion's hall,
And o'er the funeral—nuptial feaft prefide. [*Exit.*

I

SCENE III. Enter TRISTRAM, *armed with fword and Target; The* SENESCHAL, *and a* SEWER.

Trift. And fo we are to have feafting before fighting? mafter Senefchal!

Senefchal. Aye—and good reafons there be, mafter Newcomer.

Trift. Aye—I hope the Raifins are good, mafter Senefchal, or they will make an ill part of the defert. But, for reafons lefs eatable, which be they?

Sen. They be three in number, mafter Newcomer.

Trift. Hem!—Three!—But three is a favourite number, I believe, among you Scandinavians.

Sen. True, mafter Newcomer—and for good reafon. It is myftical and facred. For example—there be three fons of Beör (Woden, Vile, and Ve) who knock'd the giant Ymer o' the head, created the world out of his carcafe, and fet his brains a flying thro the air for clouds.

Trift. Hum!—A hum! I can fmell it. *(Afide.)*—A pretty piece of flefh, at this rate, your Ymer muft have been, mafter Senefchal.—And yet, upon fecond thoughts, he was but a moody, muddy, addle-headed fort of a giant, either; or his brains could not have been converted to fuch a ufe.

Sen. Then there be three Fatal Sifters.

Trift. Aye—three Witches, as one might fay, mafter Senefchal! the eldeft of which, by the way, is no Witch, i' my way of thinking; for fhe only foretells what is paft: carrying her eyes behind her, as it were.

Strait forward fhe cannot fee fo far as her nofe. And, as for the fecond, (by your account of her) fhe has no more forefight than a hare: and yet, fhe feems more indebted to her eyes than her underftanding for her reputation in the world. Her glances go, bolt fhot, in all directions, thro all impediments of fpace and matter: like a lance thro a battered buckler. She can fee all the blemifhes that a maid hides with her mantle, or a batchelor under his gabardine, as plain as a carbuncle on a nofe of four inches; but as for how long the batchelor fhall remain a batchelor, or the maid a maid, mafter Senefchal!—

Sen. Why for that, mafter Newcomer, fhe refers you to her younger fifter. And this, by the way, brings me, pat, to three other Sifters, of a very different defcription, (not but they, alfo, have fomething to do with our deftinies, mafter Newcomer!) I mean the three fmirking damfels, that wait on The Propitious Goddefs, to whom the aforefaid maids and batchelors offer up their vows, when they wifh to be maids and batchelors no longer.

And then there be three Giants of Froft; three War-hounds, that guard the Gates of Hela; and three Valkyries, that wait on the banquet of Woden, in Valhalla.

Sewer. Very true, mafter Senefchal: but what has all this to do with the reafons for our banquet?

Sen. Why much, mafter Sewer:—much.

Trift. Aye, very much, mafter Sewer: for a Banquet is a Banquet, whether in Valhalla or Gwrtheyrnion: Is it not? mafter Senefchal! There's affinity, for you, imprimus. Then, in the fecond place—for we can find three affinities, or fimilitudes, in this cafe, alfo—Can we not? mafter Senefchal!—In the fecond place, a full ftomach is better than an empty one, in Gwrtheyrnion as well as in Valhalla—Is it not, mafter Senefchal? There's affinity for you, again, or the devil's in it. And then, in the third place, (which brings us to our point;) there are three reafons for the banquet, in one place, as well as the other—videlicit—there be victuals to eat—there be people to eat them—and there is a place in which they may be eaten. Which, alfo, may in three diverfe ways be ftated—to wit, Imprimus, The paffivity, or the victuals eatable—the locality, or the place of eating—and the agency, or the perfons to eat. Secundo, The promptitude, or defire of eating—the aptitude, or convenience of a place to eat in—and the plentitude, or abundance of things eatable. Tertio, Yearning of the bowels, or the hungering after—temptation to the eye, or the prefence of the things whereafter we hunger—and miniftration copulative; or the tables and benches, in the great hall; whereby the parties are enabled to approximate, the come-at-ability of the defired is facilitated, and the defirers are fundamentally accommodated.

Sen. Right! right! mafter Newcomer! Truly, for all thou beeft a Welchman, and I a Saxon, I defire thy further acquaintance; for thou feemeft learned in thefe matters, and of an excellent wit.

Sew. Why now, by your leave, mafter Senefchal, all thefe be good reafons for banqueting at all times—but they be no reafons for banqueting before battle.

Sen. Short—fhort, mafter Sewer. If they be good reafons for banqueting at all times, then be they good reafons for banqueting before, as well as after.

Sew. Aye; but the fpecific, mafter Senefchal! the fpecific.

Trift. Why the fpecifics be three, alfo, mafter Sewer. Imprimus—there is fifh to be eaten; and they are beft to be eaten frefh—Secundo, fighting is hard work; and good eating and drinking minifter to ftrength—Tertio, it is thought beft to eat firft, left a part of the guefts fhould get their bellies fo full of fighting, as to have no appetite left for any thing elfe.

Sen. And, if thefe tripple reafons fatisfy not the tender confcience, there is yet behind, a reafon omnipotent, which is one and indivifible; namely, that The Fates would have it fo.

Trift. The Fates! How fo? mafter Senefchal.

Sen. Why, to tell you a fecret—our miftrefs has been making a journey into hell.

Trift. (*afide.*) Aye, aye, to befpeak apartments I fuppofe.—Hum!

Sen. And, as fhe reports it, The Fatal Sifters ordered this banquet.

Trift. Did they fo? Faith I fhall have a better opinion of them, for the future, than I ufed to have.

Sew. Aye, and fo fhall I. Od zookers! I cared not if our Miftrefs went to hell every day, at this rate.

Sen. It is neceffary, it feems, that the reconciliation between her and the King fhould be thus celebrated; and that, in token of their re-union, fhe fhould prefent him with a Cup of her own mixing; as fhe did at their firft meeting; and then all is to go well.

Sew. Good! mafter Senefchal. And yet our priefts will have it that it is not orthodox : becaufe, in Valhalla, Woden and his Monoheroes always fight firft, and banquet afterwards.

Trift. Aye, aye !—they want one half of us to get a quietus before the banquet, that there may be a double fhare of the baked and boiled for them. But as for thofe Monoheroes, I have a fong about them : and, if the harpers and trumpeters will bear me out with an accompaniment, I care not if I fing it to you.

O ! your joys of Valhalla to me they are all mere
      Greek, Sirs,
Where you fight till you are kill'd—

   [Kill'd ?—well : and what of that ? If it were but once,
      and away, one would not mind it—(&c. &c. *ad*
      libitum.) But there—why

There you're kill'd and kill'd again, every day of the
      Week, Sirs !
And after that, you get fo drunk that you fcarcely can
      fpeak, Sirs,
        And thefe are the joys of Valhalla !

There ten-hundred-times ten-thoufand, Sirs, as I am
      a finner,
Hack, and hew, and thruft, for fun—

   [O very pretty fun, to be fure—Here a leg, and
      there an arm ; and there a little fcratch ; juft thro
      the fcull to the chin ; and there a head off, whifp !
      —(&c. &c.) for thus

They hack, and hew, and thruſt, for fun; and both
　　the loſer and the winner
Are cut up juſt like pork, ere they ſet them down
　　to dinner.
　　　　Theſe, theſe are the joys of Valhalla!

Then for knives they uſe their ſwords, and for forks
　　they uſe their lances,
And their ſhields are turned to platters——

　　[Aye, leave them alone for good ſpacious trenchers.
　　　Their hacking and hewing, and cutting and thruſt-
　　　ing, get them a good appetite, I'll warrant——A
　　　chine of beef, a gooſe, and a turkey, are nothing
　　　under a Monohero's doublet——and ſo

Their ſhields are turn'd to platters; and a thouſand
　　ſuch like fancies,
And a Death's head, for a goblet, their drink very much
　　enhances.
　　　　Theſe, theſe are the joys of Valhalla!

Now your eating I have ſome, and your drinking
　　much delight in;
And I've no great objeƈtion to your tilting and
　　your fighting——

　　[No, it ſhall be ſeen, by-and-by, that, ſword and
　　　target, cut and thruſt, hack and hew, here a
　　　head, and there a limb, (&c. &c.) little Triſtram
　　　will play his part with the beſt of you:

For I've no great objeƈtion to your tilting and your
　　fighting;

But as to getting drunk after being kill'd,———
 Why, that I think, they're not right in.
  Altho 'tis the joy of Valhalla!

Then their MODUS BIBENDI, to me, it is mightily
  droll, Sirs,
And the scull of a foe, is a very strange sort of a
  waffail-bowl, Sirs—

[O, lud! I'm all in the horrors to think of it.
 Who the devil could set himself soberly to work
 to get drunk, with a death's-head in his hand? Be-
 fides how the devil do they manage it?

For the scull of a foe is such a very strange sort of a
  bowl, Sirs,
That I am very sure I should spill———out at either
  eye-hole, Sirs,
  Ere it got to my mouth in Valhalla!

Then give me still a banquet of your mere mortal
  cooking—

[Nay, no cooking at all—Radishes and raw turnips;
 an apple, and an onion—or a good Welch leek
 (&c. &c.) in a thatched cottage, rather than chines
 and turkies, in your Hall of Shields—

Yes, give me still a dinner of such plain vulgar cooking;
And ere ale in a scull, I'll drink Adam's ale the brook in:
And, if there's any other heaven I can find a sly nook in,
  I'll be damn'd if I'll go to Valhalla!
                                    [*Exeunt.*

SCENE IV. A confufed and tumultuous noife within.
Shrieks, and a cry of help.—A deep groan is heard
Enter feveral GUESTS *and* SERVANTS, *flying, to and*
fro, acrofs the ftage, in terror and aftonifhment.
Dirgeful mufic, from the Harps, within.

Enter ROWENNA, *in great agitation.* EDELTHRED.
      AGGA, *&c. following.*

Row. 'Tis done !—'Tis done !—The charm is bound :
   Vortigern his fleep profound
         Has quaft. *(A groan within.)*
He dies ! *(a groan.)* He dies ! *(a groan.)* He dies !
For this below (with half-thaw'd eyes)
   Icy Hela, fhouting, laught. *(Groan again.)*
         He dies ! he dies !
To the Nine-fold Realm he hies—
   Mifty region !—cold, and dark !
         Hark !————
Grymer leads the tripple growl.
Now they open. Now they howl. *(Barking below.)*
   Hark ! *(Barking)* Hark ! *(Barking)* Hark !
   Loud the ravening hell-dogs bark.
Fenrir fhakes his chains below :
They yell !—the Giant Sons of Woe !—
And wide the creeking portals throw.
         Hark !————
   Clank of chains, and growl, and bark——
Hideous difcord ! *(Clank of chains)* Hark ! *(A deep*
       growl) Hark ! *(barking)* Hark !——
Ed. Ag. &c. Hideous difcord ! Hark ! hark ! hark !
  K

Accompaniments of barking, howling, &c. Then, a solemn pause; and a sudden transition to soft and melancholy music; principally of Harps and Flutes.
The BODY OF VORTIGERN *is carried across the stage, accompanied by* COURTIERS, DOMESTICS, SOLDIERS, *&c. &c. while* THE BARDS *sing the following dirge.*

> Mourn, Britons, mourn the mighty fall'n :
>   The sceptred hand is cold.
> The imperial brow in duft lies low,
>   By sudden Fate controll'd.
> Mourn, Britons, mourn the mighty fall'n :
>   The sceptred hand is cold !

             [*Exeunt with the Body.*

ROWENNA *(after a pause.)*
Why should this moody dirge, these solemn sounds
Of grief-full mockery, and this apish train,
That mourn but by contagion from the harps
Of hireling choristers, infect my eyes,
Or chill my veins with horror ?—Up ! to arms,
Ye firm Resolves ! and fortify my soul
Against invading Conscience. True, he sleeps—
Sleeps with the dead !—my some-time plighted lord—
By me, he sleeps his death. But Fate's, not mine,
Is all the guilt—if guilt. The Fates decreed,
And I but did their biddings.—But a wife ?———
A wife !—Away : I never was the wife
Of such a thing as Vortigern. My soul
(That scorns affiance with the low and vile)

Wedded not him, but Empire; and to that
I ſtill am true and loyal: making way,
By this predeſtin'd act, for happier rule,
And a more worthy maſter.   Arthur's hand
Shall heal thy griefs, and mine — Heav'n-favour'd Iſle!
And congregated Britain bleſs the deed.

Join, then, the chaunt to Frea. Frea now,
Propitious Goddeſs! may accept the vow;
To her, and Gna, ſwell ſoft the melting ſtrains—
For theirs what yet of deſtiny remains.

Queen of Pleaſures! Queen of Smiles!
Goddeſs of reſiſtleſs wiles,
And Love's extatic glow!
Thou, who, erſt, the golden tear
Shed'ſt o'er Balder's early bier,
And felt'ſt the touch of tender woe—
Propitious Goddeſs! hear.

Ed. Ag. &c.   Queen of Love's extatic glow—
Propitious Goddeſs! hear.

Row.   O! ſend the herald of thy will,
The throbbings of the heart to ſtill,
And whiſper Peace and love!
The imperfect work of Fate complete,
Till ſigh with ſigh, reſponſive, meet:
O! firſt of genial powers above!
Propitious Goddeſs! hear.

Ed. Ag. &c.   Firſt of genial powers above!——
Propitious Goddeſs! hear.

Trumpets, without, and a cry of The foe! The foe!
   A L W I N *enters, with great precipitation.*

Alw. Moſt noble Queen! Arthur has gain'd the heights.
His trumpet ſounds defiance at our gates;
And down the ſteep, to this our mid-way ſtrand,
His ſhouting legion pours: their banner'd vans
Chiding, with fluttering ſpeed, the buoyant air;
Like wings of eagles, when they downward ruſh
To pounce their ſhrieking prey.
                Row. Hang out the flag
Of friendly parley.   This is welcome news.
The tyrant's death makes way for gentler warfare —
More mild arbitriment than ſlings and darts:
And this ſhall firſt be tried.

     Enter a ſecond M E S S E N G E R.

        Meſſenger.   Revolt! revolt!
Treaſon is in our walls; a treacherous band
Of lawleſs Britons, headed by the twain,
Who, with their proffer'd ſervice, late arriv'd,
Have borne the Princeſs to the lonely tower,
By ſudden inroad ſeiz'd, and now maintain'd
In Arthur's hoſtile name.
      Row. (eagerly.) The lonely tower?
   Meſ. The ſame that, circled by the deep-delv'd moat,
Stands inſulated: leſs by taҍic art,
Than by the never-ceaſing ſpring, that laves
Its circular baſe, defended.
       Row. Fire the bridge!——

This news is welcome too.   My fates prevail!—
No weapons use but fire.—Propitious powers!
Ye faithful Fatal Sisters!——Shaft and sling
Were sacrilegious here; were impotent.
Fire, fire, I say.   The first that brings me word
The turrets flame (be he the meanest drudge
That ever pioneer'd before a host)
Shall rank, for wealth and power, with Woden's line.

Exeunt ALW. and MES.

Yes!——" My rival to confound,
 " Fire and water shall surround—
 " Ruthless flames, and waves profound!"

Sweet Hope my heart beguiles:
My bosom swells—my pulse beats high;
And softer heaves the fluttering sigh.

Propitious Frea smiles!   Exeunt.

*SCENE V. The outside of the Castle, situated half way
up the Beacons; at that part now occupied by the Lake
or Pool.   The double peak of the Mountain forms the
back ground.   The Keep, or round Tower, appears
detached from the rest of the fortification; and sur-
rounded by a wide moat.   The drawbridge, between it
and the Castle is drawn up; and* TRISTRAM *and*
GUENEVER *are seen upon the Walls.   The other
parts of the Castle are, also, defended by a moat; the
drawbridge being up.   A perpetual shower of fire-
brands is discharged, from the Castle, upon the Keep.*

TRISTRAM *(hurling back the brands, as they are thrown.)*
Fire for your fire, ye Salamanders! if that's your game.
But here comes one will fire you prettily; I'll warrant.

Trumpet-Chorus of BARDS *and* KNIGHTS, *as* ARTHUR,
and his Train are entering.

Trumpets founding, falchions flaming!
Rush, ye chiefs to glorious fight:
Fame, the while, your worth proclaiming ——

Arth. Destruction!—See upon the keep (surpris'd
By Tristram's politic valour, to secure,
During our fierce assault, from chance of war,
Or worse internal treason, the fair prize
Of all our sleepless perils) what fierce shower
Of hellish engin'ry, incessant, hails,
Threat'ning a fate of horrors. Sound the trump—
The trump of parley.—Guenever!

   Guenever.   Oh! heav'n!
Arthur! my lord! my hero!—in thy fight——
O! cruel destiny!

  Arth. The trumpet found. [*A parley founded.*
If maid, or child, or matron they would save
From retributive vengeance, let them cease
This war of fire;

(ROWENNA, *attended by* ALWIN, *and feveral* SAXON
and BRITISH NOBLES, *&c. appears on the walls.*)

    or, by the Eternal Truth,
Whom my foul worships! foon Gwrtheyrnion's walls,

Proftrate on earth, fhall form one common tomb
For every Saxon thing that breathes within;
And thefe my gallant knights, horribly fmear'd
With your idolatrous blood, fhall, o'er the heap
Of mingled wreck and carnage, wave their fwords,
And fhout " Extermination !"

      Row. Angry prince !
Why to our flag of conference anfwer you
With fuch ungentle outrage ? Were we bent
On hoftile fury, we have means within
To baffle this gay phalanx ; tho renown'd,
(As frankly we admit) for warlike deeds,
Thro all the peopled earth. But, in our hearts,
The touch humane of cordial fympathy
Is now more vital than revengeful wrath
And national averfions ; which too long
Have thin'd our rival tribes. Therefore we arm
Our tongues with gentle courtefies, not hands
With weapons of deftruction ; and invite
To equal brotherhood your warrior Knights—
Yourfelf, to equal empire.

     Arth. Empire, fhar'd
With Vortigern and thee ?

      Row. That Vortigern
No more prefents a barrier to the hopes
Of Anglia and of Britain : cold he lies
Beneath the frefh-laid turf ; and, with his fleep,
The bleeding realm is pacified.

     Arth. How ?—How ?—

Did I then prophecy? Moſt murderous fiend!
Thy huſband, and thy ſovereign!
                              Row. Why on me
(Injurious!) charge the ſure decrees of Fate?
    Arth. Fate, that would deal in murders and in crimes,
Shall never want (while thou infeſt'ſt the earth)
A ready inſtrument.   No more.   Break off
The impious parle.   The martial chorus raiſe;
And let our battering enginery upheap,
Of theſe polluted ſtones, a monument
To Britain's murder'd King: foul tho he were,
Of theſe, not meriting ſo foul an end.

    Cho. Trumpets ſounding, falchions flaming,
            Ruſh, ye Chiefs, to glorious fight——

A BRITON *(from the Walls.)*
    A while forbear!——For what do we contend?
For what deform the enamell'd turf of peace
With our unnatural ſlaughters? Arthur, hear—
Rowenna, and the undiſputed crown
Of Britain and the auxilliar tribes of Elb,
Are thine, without a crime.
                        Arth. Without a crime,
Vile Briton!—This from thee, whoſe King, even now
(Your own eleƈted King!) in death lies low
By her abhor'd contrivance!—Without crime?
Is it no crime to league with Murder, then—
Domeſtic Murder, Witchcraft, and the rage
Of foul adultrous Luſt, and all the ſwarm
Of moſt abhor'd pollutions, that combine

In her deteſted nature, and infect
The very air ſhe breathes in ?—making all
That come within thy atmoſphere of crimes,
As hateful as thyſelf—thou, World of Sins !
Guilt's fair, yet foul epitome !

     Row. Ye Gods
Of Aſgard and of Niſlheim ! is it thus
Ye cheat my hopes ?

      Yet, fair ! He owns me fair !
That's ſomething.   And, perchance, when yonder witch
No more with philtering charms can drug the ſenſe,
I may ſeem fair alone ; and, rivalry
No more obtruding, the impaſſion'd touch
Of Nature's ſtrong propenſion may ſubdue
This pride of ethic reaſon.   The loos'd eye
Of youthful appetite, that, 'mong the forms
Of ſoft obtruſive beauty, ſomewhere muſt
Dwell with more ardent gaze, from mine, perchance,
May catch contagious fire ; and Arthur yet
Light up the flame in which my woes expire. *(Aſide.)*

 Why ceaſe the brands, ye tardy miniſters
Of our imperial mandate ? Who again,
(Command who will) till yonder turrets flame,
Does in the fiery warfare but relax,
The pains of Treaſon wait him.

    (The aſſault on the Keep is renewed.)
ARTHUR *(who, during the foregoing ſoliloquy, had*
  converſed with GUENEVER, *acroſs the moat, in*
  dumb ſhow.) Quick—repeal
That hideous mandate ; or, by utmoſt hell,

  L

Whate'er of torment human wit can frame—
Whate'er of ignominy (torturous more
To thy imperious fpirit) fhall avenge
The damned deed.

     What? ha! No refpite? Fiends!
Sound—found the trumpet. Peal the affailing hymn,
Ye bards, and rufh to combat. (*The affault begins*).

Chorus. Trumpets founding, falchions flaming,
   Rufh, ye chiefs! to glorious fight:
  Fame, the while, your worth proclaiming,
   Thro the nations wings her flight.
    Rufh to conqueft! rufh to glory!
    Like the brave of ancient ftory.
  Trumpets founding, falchions flaming,
   Rufh to conqueft—rufh to glory!

The BARDS *join in the conflict. The drawbridge of the
Caftle falls; and that of the Keep, together with the
Keep itfelf, is fired, at the fame time. Shouts and
flourifh, as of triumph, from both parties.*

Arth. The drawbridge falls. Affail! affail the gates.
Diftraction!—Guenever!
    Guenever. Oh, Arthur! Arthur!
They reach—they fcorch me. O, the flames! the flames!
Arth. My arm avails not. Conqueft is in vain!
Diftraction! vengeance!—O, fome vaft revenge!
Some mighty ruin!—that the world might crack,
And Univerfal Nature, with her wreck,
Hood yon devouring flames!

             Row. The Phœnix burns!
And, from the odorous ruin, mine the love,
With renovated wing, fhall foar aloft,
Gorgeous in natal triumph.——'Tis complete. (*Afide.*)

      Schulda, thanks! The charm is bound.
      Now, my rival to confound,
      Fire and water both furround.

      Arthur's arm no help fhall lend,
      No mortal power the Maid befriend,
      Nor aid from pitying heaven defcend.

      Schulda thanks! My doubts retire.
      Arthur foon fhall light the fire
      In which my forrows all expire.

    Arth. A brand! A brand! Hell-hag—thy prophecy
(Whatever juggling demon gave it fhape)
Soon I fulfil. Triftram, a brand! a brand!

Tristram *throws feveral brands to* Arthur *and
the* Knights: Rowenna *flarts, with a terrific
fhriek, as they feize, and brandifh them on high.*

    Row. Furies of Hela's fhades! Is this the flame?
    Arth. Oh! Guenever! thus at thy funeral pyre,
I offer up thy hecatombs. Come on,
If not for prefervation, we are arm'd
At leaft for vengeance. Hell-hag! thus I light
The fated flame in which thy woes expire.

He fires the Gates; and prefently the whole caftle ap-
pears to be in flames, in the midft of which ROWENNA
and her partizans fink. In the mean time, the flames
make a more feeble progrefs in the Keep; where
GUENEVER *and* TRISTRAM *ftand.*

       AIR *and* CHORUS *of unfeen Spirits.*
       She fhrieks!—She dies!—Our miftrefs dies!
         Spirits—Spirits!—hafte away:
       Scatter thro the lurid fkies.
         Asi's Gods in pow'r decay.
       Demon Gods confefs, with fear,
       Their fated twilight hovering near.

Ar. Vengeance! thy dues are paid. But Love! O, Love!
Haft thou no intereft at The Mercy Seat?——
Nor fuffering Innocence?———My Guenever!
       (SHE *difappears and* TRISTRAM *follows.*)
Oh! torment!—torment! Thus, before mine eyes!—
Not even the wretched privilege referv'd
To perifh with her—in one dear embrace
Forget the fearching fury of the flames,
And mix our wedded afhes!   Might one not,
Of defperate refolution, make a bridge
Enough fubftantial for a lover's weight,
Buoy'd by fuch dire extremity? At leaft,
We'll try the hazard. Ho! for Guenever!

[*He runs towards the moat, which he is about to leap;*
when fuddenly the whole pile of building, Caftle and
Keep together, and all the ground they occupied, fink

down. The space becomes filled by a pool of Water. In the place where the round tower stood, The Lady of the Lake *appears in her chariot, with* Guen-ever *seated by her side, and* Tristram *behind. The Chariot, &c approaches the shore.* Scout *comes swimming after.* Arthur *and* Guenever *rush into each other's arms.*

Arth. All-gracious powers!

> *Guen.* My hero!

> > *Arth.* O! My Love!

Trist. (*springing upon land*) Huzza! Huzza! Didn't I tell you little Tristram would fight his way thro it. If there was no help from Heaven above, or the Earth beneath, there was some in the Waters that are under the earth, my blinking prophetess!

Why, how now, Scout?—What, my amphibious! my water-spaniel! You've had enough of the draught of temperance, I hope. This comes of your fears and precautions. If you had drank valiant Cwrw, as I do, and stood, to the last, at the post of danger—why you had arrived on Terra Firma, with dry breeches, my boy.

Arth. And is it realis'd?—And art thou safe?—
Safe and unhurt, from those devouring flames
That threaten'd thy chaste beauties?

> > *Guen.* Free! Unhurt!—
Save in thy frantic terrors!—There I bleed——
Here—in this storm-rent bosom. (*Laying her hand upon
his heart.*)   *Arth.* 'Tis at rest:
If blessedness be rest.——O, sacred power
Of flame-defying Chastity!—And thou! (*To the Fairy.*

Lady. See, Arthur, fee! to crown your matchlefs worth,
Nature relents, and miracles have birth,
The tribute fpring that wont its courfe to take,
Thro fecret veins, to feed my broader Lake,
A lake itfelf now fpreads at my command,
And long, an emblem of your Fame, fhall ftand,
An alpine wonder in the Cambrian land.
Meantime accept, from two-fold dangers freed,
This beauteous maid, your Valour's nobleft meed.

Beauty, Truth, and Innocence,
　　Sweetly blending all their charms,
Valour's guerdon, I difpenfe:
　　Take them, Hero, to thy arms.
Virtue with fuch Graces blending,
'Twas a prize well worth contending:
　　Worth thy perils, toils, alarms:
　　Take her, hero, to thy arms:—
Feaft of Reafon! feaft of Senfe!
Beauty, Truth, and Innocence.

Chorus. Valour true to Virtue's fide,
　　Worth, by fharp affliction tried,
　　Merit well the blooming bride
On whom propitious Fates difpenfe
Beauty, Truth, and Innocence.

Arth. O! facred Guardian!—But all words are weak:
I can but figh my raptures; gaze my thanks,
And, in the precious gift, the giver prize.

Tali. Trumpet's clangors, Arms that rattle,
Dreadful thro the bleeding battle,
                    Now, a while,
    For kindling Beauty's rofeate fmile—
        Soothing foftnefs! we forego.
        Hafte Thee, Love! the wreath beftow.
                Witching fmile
                And fportive wile
    That fenfe of wearied worth beguile;
        And Stelth, that love's coy nectar fips;
        And tilt and toy of parrying lips;
        Eyes that fwim; and hearts that glow;
        And parly with the yielding foe;—
        Thefe, for laurels, Love! beftow;
And we again will fight thy battle.

Bard. Hafte thee, Boy! But wing thy arrows
    With the dove's plume; not the fparrow's:
        Turtle, that, in thickeft grove,
        Guards the neft of abfent love.
        And ftill, as Valour's meed, difpenfe
        Beauty, Truth, and Innocence.
    So, when ftorms of danger rattle,
    We again will fight thy battle.

Chorus. Beauty, Truth, and Innocence
        Still, as Valour's meed difpenfe;
    And, when ftorms of danger rattle,
    Valour's fons fhall fight thy battle.

Lady. But fee below, how from the mifty vale
The day retires, and twilight fhades prevail.
Soon fhall thofe fhadows up the mountain fpread,
And Night involve Farinioch's peaky head.
One thing remains: to waft my chofen fon
To Caër Leon: then my tafk is done.
There Britain's chiefs affembled, even now,
Prepare the regal fillet for thy brow.
Ye fightlefs agents of the charmed air!
Suftain our weight.   Behold: for we are there.

*SCENE VI. She waves her filver Trident, and the
fcene changes to Caer-Leon, in all its fabled grandeur;
fplendidly illuminated, and decorated with martial
trophies, banners, wreaths, and braids of flowers,
aud other fumptuous preparations for the coronation of
ARTHUR. NOBLES, BARDS, LADIES, YOUTHS,
and MAIDENS with bafkets of Flowers, MASKERS,
REVELLERS, &c.*

La. Here youths and maids your gather'd fragrance fling:
Behold your promis'd Chief—your patriot King.

*The Youths and Maidens ftrew their flowers; and the
Chiefs, &c. prefent the regal fillet to ARTHUR, who
binds it on the brow of GUENEVER.*

Tal. Hail Britain's pride! immortal Arthur hail!
Thy honour, name, and praife fhall never fail!
  Cho. Hail Britain's pride! immortal Arthur hail!
Thy honour, name, and praife fhall never fail!

Lady. Thus cóver'd with glory, thus bleſt in thy love,
To empire promoted, thy virtue to prove,
Forget not that worth, in the funſhine of joy,
That griefs could not quench, or afflictions annoy.
Let your valour protect, but not ravage the ſtate;
And cheriſh the Low, while you rule o'er the great;
So the bard, yet unborn, ſhall your triumphs proclaim,
And the nations around thus re-echo your Fame—
" Hail Britain's pride! immortal Arthur, hail!
" Your honour, name, and praiſe ſhall never fail."
Chorus. Hail Britain's pride! &c.—

Talies.   Wake the Harp to ſtrains of pleaſure!
       Let the ſportive train advance:
       Ring of ſhields, and pyrrhic meaſure!
       Warriors, lead the nuptial dance.

A Dance of Warriors.

War and Toil have done their duty:
       Let your weary'd worth repoſe.
Love ſucceeds; and ſmiling Beauty,
       With our laurel twines the roſe.

A Dance of Virgins who crown ARTHUR *and his*
KNIGHTS *with chaplets.*

Chorus. Love and Glory, thus uniting,
       All their mingled boons confer.
     Arthur, lo! thy worth requiting,
       Empire, Fame, and Guenever.

M

Lady.   Now, my tafk perform'd, I fly
To my fecret bowers, that lie
Where the Day-Star never came,
         Peering——Fleering,
With his fearching eye of flame.
There, in virgin ftate, I rove
Thro' fparry dome, and coral grove,
Self-illum'd with many a Gem
Might grace a monarch's diadem.

Refponfe below, as the Chariot rifes.

     Lady! Lady! hafte to rove
Thro' fparry dome and coral grove.
See your Swans their traces fhake,
Regent of the filver lake!

Lady.   There, where bubbling fonts arife
And the blue-eye'd Naides
Thro the chinks, in many a rill,
         Tinkling——Sprinkling,
Their falubrious boons diftill—
There I join the virgin throng,
Warbling oft the choral fong
That brooks and echoing falls repeat,
To Fancy's ear, in numbers fweet.

Refponfe of Nymphs below.

     Lady! Lady! hafte along:
Join the Choir, and join the fong;
       Gurgling—tinkling,
       Murmuring—fprinkling,
Sadly fweet, the rocks among.

Lady, as she seats herself in the Chariot.

　　Sifters, I the call obey,
　　Seek the Grot, and join the lay;
　　　　Murmuring—tinkling,
　　　　Bubbling—fprinkling,
　　Where the chryftal fountains,
　　　　　From their mountains,
　　　　　　Gufhing—Rufhing,
To their vallies hafte away.

TALIESSIN.

May thofe fountains, Lady kind!
Still their wonted channels find,
Nor ever water-nymph negleét
The filent tribute of refpeét,
But, thro many a fecret vein,
Still the purer effence ftrain,
And thy myftic urn fupply;
Never turbid, never dry:—
Urn fo pure, that Lunvey's tide,
Thro its waters doom'd to glide,
Silent, with unmingling wave,
Haftes the wooddy glen to lave,
And there, to lift'ning groves, complains
Of Love o'eraw'd, and ftifled pains;
With virgin beauties aye embrac'd,
Which yet he muft not hope to tafte.
May ever on thy brink appear
The earlieft fragrance of the year,

And lingering Autumn in thy face
Reflected fee his lateft grace;
While ftill, as circling hours prevail,
The matin Lark and Nightingale
The fong of lengthen'd rapture wake
To hail the Lady of the Lake.

CHORUS.

Blow the martial trump again,
Give to Fame the clofing ftrain—
Fame, that fhall her wreaths confer
On Arthur and on Guenever;
And bid her loudeft clarion wake,
To hail the Lady of the Lake.

THE CURTAIN DROPS.

FAIRY OF THE LAKE.

ACT I, Sc. I. p. 3. *Invisible Spirits.* The Laplanders continue to this day to believe in a sort of Demons of the Air, (called Jeuhles) who inhabit the air and have great power over human actions; but are without form or substance. *Guthr. Gramm. p. 97, 9th Edit.—Sheffer's Hist. Lapland, Ch. 9, &c.*

V. 3. *With Runic Spell.* The northern nations held their Runic verses in such reverence, that they believed them sufficient (provided they were pronounced with great emotion of mind—together with a firm belief) to raise the ghosts of the departed. *Five Pieces of Runic Poetry from the Icelandic, p. 6. Percy's Reliques, &c.*

V. 5. *Pride of Woden's race,* Woden (or Odin) was the Scandinavian God of War—the Chief and Father of all the other Gods. From him all the Saxon princes affected to trace their descent. *See the Genealogical Tables in Rapine, Vol. I. B. 3.* Once for all, both in this Drama, and in the Hope of Albion, I have followed the suggestion of Milton (and, indeed, of The Old and New Testament) in considering these Demon Gods as real personages—as rebellious and fallen angels assuming these forms to draw the deluded nations into idolatry,

V. 13. *The misty realms of Frost.* The Hell of the Scandinavians was a frozen region, involved in perpetual mists, and hail, and snow, and sleet. To this region, The Dysæ—(avenging Goddesses,) or messengers of Woden, delivered over the Ghosts of perjurers and cowards, and all who did not die in battle, or by some violent death; there to be tormented with hunger, thirst, and all sorts of evils. *Univ. Hist.; Mallet's North, Antiq.; Cottle's Edda; Sayers; &c.*

P. 4. v. 1. *The Fatal Sisters.* The destinies, who were believed to weave for every individual a mysterious web, upon which their fate depended. They are, sometimes, called *Nornies*; and with them, sometimes, are confounded the Dysæ.

V. 2. *Hela.* The Goddess of Death; or Queen of the infernal regions. She was the Daughter of Lok (the Evil Spirit) and of Signa or Sinna (whence the word Sin) his Spouse. All the race of Lok were evil, and hostile to the other Gods. *Cottle, &c.* and *Eng. Encyclop. Art. Mythology.*

V. 5. *Valhalla.* The Hall-of-Shields — Woden's palace, where the Monoheroes or Patriarchs, engaged every day in direful conflict; after which they sat down to regale themselves at a sumptuous banquet, and drank ale and wassail, &c. out of the sculls of their enemies. *See any of the authorities above quoted.*

V. 8. *Frea.* The Goddess of Beauty (Daughter of Niord, or Nocca, God of the Sea.) She was the wife of Woden—tho Sayer and some others assign that honour to Hertha—I believe upon no better authority than Tacitus: who, certainly, upon Runic Mythology, is not a very good one. She is called "the " propitious Goddess;" and to her lovers prefer their vows.

Ibid. Asgardian Bowers. Asgard is the heaven of the Scandinavians.

V. 4. from bottom. *Asori's Gods.* Woden and his race are called the Asi or Asori. This term, properly speaking, includes all the northern Deities but Nocca, who, tho ranked among the Gods, was not of the Asori race.

P. 5. v. 9. *Schulda.* The youngest of the Destinies but the most awful. She presides over the future.

V. 11. *Braga.* The God of Eloquence, of Poetry, and Music.

V. 12. *Asamael.* The Language of Poetry. As the word Runic, strictly speaking, is applicable only to the character in which the verses of the Northern Poets (or Scalds) were written, so is Asamael descriptive of the particular dialect in which their poetry was always composed.

P. 6. v. 5. *Ensanguined Altars.* Human victims (especially prisoners of war) were offered to Woden, and others of these Demon Gods.

V. 9. *Cloud-compelling Thor.* The God of Thunder, or of the Air: Son of Woden and Frea. With his iron gauntlet he hurled the thunder-bolts; and with his mace he controuled the Giants of Frost, and ruled the elements. He was also a great warrior; the adversary of the gigantean race; and the victor of Lok, and all his monster-brood.

P. 7. v. 1. *Mara.* The Spectre who oppresses and terrifies people in their sleep. Hence " Night Mara" (the Maid of Night,) by corruption, " Night Mare."

V. 12. *Cimbrian Groves.* The Saxon tribes before their migration to Britain inhabited the Cimbrica Chersonesus; a part of the present Kingdom of Denmark. *Verstegan's Rest. Ant. Chap. I.*

P. 8. v. 3. *Hertha,* or the Earth. The mother of all the Gods. The Goddess also of fertility.

V. 18. *Dread Fiend Unutterable.* The Malignant Spirit, A NAMELESS FEMALE, residing in a great house under the sea; where, by her charms and incantations, she causes dearth, by confining all the fishes, &c. of the sea. To relieve the Greenlanders from such calamities, an Angekok, or Magician, journies thro' the KINGDOM OF SOULS, over an horrible abys, to the palace of this phantom, and by his charms compels her to release them. *Crantz Hist. Greenl.*

P. 9. v. 3. (from the bottom) *Valkyries.* Subordinate Goddesses, who attend upon the Table of Woden, and usually execute his commands, selecting those in battle who are doomed to die, &c. Sometimes he mixed in the conflict, and struck the victims himself.

P. 10. v. 5. *Iduna's Banquet.* She possessed The Apples of Youth; of which, when advancing to old age, the Deities tasted, and were instantly restored to their former youth and vigour.

V. the last. *Gwertheurnion.* This castle was, in reality, situated among the fastnesses of Plynlimmon, near the source of the Wye. If the use I have made of the liberty is not unpoetical, I shall be excused for removing it to the Beacons of Brecknock (Farinioch.)

P. 14. v. 16. *The Moon withdraws his light.* In Northern Mythology, and, indeed, in most of the Northern Languages, The Sun is feminine; and the Moon masculine. *See an article, full of erudition and accurate criticism upon the subject of these notes, in the Monthly Magazine for December, 1798, p. 454. See also Beatie's Theory of Language.*

Sc. 2. P. 17. l. 12. *The Twilight of the Gods.* The Scandinavian Deities were not supposed to be immortal. They were to perish in the general wreck of the universe. This is what is called The Twilight of the Gods; and the descriptions of this, and of the predicted resuscitation of Nature from the wreck, constitute the noblest parts of the system of Runic Mythology.

SCENE 3. p. 19. l. 2. *A Female Child,* &c. The pictured Drum, used in the rites of northern magic, was a sort of Kettle Drum, hollowed out of pine, fir, or birch, and covered with a skin, painted over with a variety of mysterious characters, &c. The hammer, partly in the form of the letter Y, was made of the same sort of wood. It was kept carefully wrapt up in the skin of the Loam, a bird that always lives in the water; and it was held so sacred, that no marriageable woman might venture to approach it. For the method of using these, and the rings, images, &c. mentioned in the text—see *Sheffer's Lapland.*

V. 14. *The Bear* was not exterminated from this Island till some centuries after the time from which the action of this Drama is taken. See *note in Pennant's British Zoology.*

P. 20. v. 5. *The Night-Swallow;* Goat-Sucker, Night-Hawk, or Chum Owl. A bird of passage. It visits England about May, and returns in August. *Buffon.*

P. 21. v. 2. *Niflheim.* The Home of mists; or Frozen Hell: called, also, The Ninefold World; being subdivided into so many regions.

V. 6. *Ifing.* The River that separates the giants and race of evil beings, &c. from the Gods. The word itself means strife, or anger.

V. 7. *Thy Dome of Anguish,* &c. The palace of Hela was Anguish; her Table, Famine; her Waiters were Expectation and delay; the threshold of her door was Precipice; her bed, Leanness; she was livid and ghastly pale; and her very looks inspired horror.

V. 20. *Ymer* (or Augelmer.) He seems to be, alternately, considered as the Son of Chaos, and as Chaos itself. He is father of the race of Giants (or Jutes) i. e. of the adversaries of the Asori. He is not considered as a God, because all his race were evil. Odin, Vile, and Ve, the Sons of Bor or Bëor, slew this giant, and the blood from his wounds caused a general inundation, &c. They then carried him into the middle of Ginnungagap (the great void), where, from his flesh, they created the earth; the sea and rivers from his blood; mountains from his bones; rocks and stones from his teeth and broken bones; herbs from his hair; heaven from his scull; the habitable regions from his eyebrows; and the clouds from his brains.

P. 23. v. 4 & 5. *The Wolf-like Serpent — Midgard's Serpent.* One of the monster brood of Lok—consequently an adversary of the Gods. He was cast into the sea, there to remain till conquered, at the last day, by the God Thor, who, in his turn, is suffocated in the floods of venom, which the Dragon breathes forth, as he expires.

L. 10. *Hell-dogs' tripple growl,* The bridge and gates of hell are guarded by three dogs; of which *Grimer* is the chief. They feed on the carcases of the dead.

L. 11. *Rafaen.* The Raven of Schulda, who carries the decrees of Fate to Woden.

Ibid. *Fenrir* (or Fenris.) The Wolf. Another of the monster brood of Lok. Tyr, and the other warrior Deities bound this adversary of the Gods in chains. But these he is to burst at The Twilight of the Gods: when opening his enormous mouth, that reaches from the Earth to Heaven, he is to swallow up the Sun. Woden, in his golden casque, and resplendant cuiras, attacks him with his vast scimitar: but he is devoured; and Fenrir perishes at the same instant.

SCENE 4. P. 24, v. 13. *Lok's prolific hate.* The evil Genius of the Scandinavians; ranked, nevertheless, among their Gods. The Architect of Guilt, &c. Beautiful in figure; but surpassing all beings in perfidy and craft. He had many children.

V. 18. *By the channels twelve,* &c. Niflheim (or Nifleil) was created long before the Earth; and in the centre of which rose a fountain called Hvergelmer. Its effluvia produced many rivers near the boundary of Hell. The names of some of these were Misery, Hope deferred, Swift Perdition, Cruel Storm, Wailing and Gnashing of Teeth.

P. 25. *The Bridge where Giol rolls.* Giöl is one of the rivers of Hell. Over the bridge that crosses it the ghosts of Cowards, Perjurers, &c. pass in their way to the infernal abodes.

P. 26. v. 3 and 4. *Norrer.* The father of Night. *Dager.* Day.

P. 29. v. 2. *Hydrassil* (or Hydrasil.) The sacred Ash of Asgard. The court of the Gods is ordinarily kept under a great ash-tree; and there they distribute justice. This ash is the greatest of all trees; its branches cover the surface of the earth; its top reaches to the highest heaven; it is supported by three vast roots, one of which extends to the ninth world, or Hell. An eagle, whose piercing eye discovers all things, perches upon its branches. From under one of the roots runs a fountain where Wisdom lies concealed. From a neighbouring spring (the fountain of past things) three virgins are continually drawing a precious water, with which they water the Ash-tree: this water, after having refreshed its leaves, falls back again upon the earth, where it forms the dew of which the bees make their honey.

ACT 2. P. 32. Sc. 1. *The Lady.* The Cambrian superstitions harmonize so readily with those of the Northern nations; and the mixed and illegitimate christianity of those times borders so closely upon paganism, that, I trust, the combination will not destroy the *poetical probability* of either. The Lady of the Lake, according to Cambrian Story, was one of the Fairy guardians of Arthur. In delineating her character I should, perhaps, have been justified by the record in representing her in a very different point of view from that which I have chosen. It is no improbable conjecture that the fable originated in the mysterious seclusion of some beautiful mistress of the British Champion; and that Arthur (like the more fortunate Numa) had the art to derive the Credit of sanctity from the indulgence of an illicit amour. She was, however, considered by the ancient Cambrians as a benignant Spirit—a guardian of the just and holy cause; and with these ideas modern morality cannot reconcile the supposition of an amorous connection. Accordingly she is here represented as a personification of essential purity; and the Lake assigned as her particular residence, is rendered typical of this, by allusion to the tradition, still popular in the neighbourhood, that the Lunvey flows thro' the middle without mingling any part of its waters with those of the Lake itself.

P. 35. Sc. 2. l. 17. *Cwrw*—pronounced cooroo (for the w of the Welsh answers to our double o) is the Cambrian word for Ale.

P. 44. v. 2. Making Guenever, a daughter of Vortigern, and the object of the incestuous passion with which that tyrant has been stigmatized, is another of those liberties for which, as a Poet, I hope to be pardoned.

Ibid. Sc. 4. v. 2. *Balder's Steed, with reinless neck.* Balder was one of the sons of Woden; and guided the Horse of the Sun (for the Gods of the Scandinavians were not chariotteers, but equestrians.) He was killed with a branch of mistletoe, by his brother Hoder, thro' the malice of Lok; and, not dying in battle, descended to the Regions of Hela.

P. 46. v. 16. *The Bird of Peace.* The Heitre: a Bird of calm: the Halcyon of the North.

P. 47. *Twin Heights of bleak Fariniock*. The double peak of the Beacons, Vans, or heights of Brecknock.

V. 17. *Perchance the Maid*, &c. Gna; the Messenger of Frea, and one of the 3 Handmaids or Graces of this northern Venus.

P. 51. v. 11. *Demons of the Sultry Noon*. Northern Superstition has its Demons of Noon, as well as its Elves of Night. They are of the male sex, and are an evil and malignant race. Their abode is in Alfheim. St. Bazil recommends us to pray to God some time before noon to avert the danger to be apprehended from Demons of this description.

P. 61. *Thee—fire-eyed Seraph !* &c. This and the following Ode are addressed to the Tutelary Angel of Albion, or Britain. That the belief of such supernatural Agencies, presiding over different tribes, nations, states, provinces, cities, &c. is a consistent part of the christian faith, may be shewn by several passages from the Book of Daniel, and, indeed, from several other parts of the Scriptures. It forms the basis of an essential part of the Machinery of "The Hope of Albion."

ACT 3. Sc. 2. p. 65. v. 12. *Sisters three*, &c. The Valkyries. See former note.

Sc. 3. p. 67. l. 20. *Three Giants of Frost*. I do not know that their number is so limitted. But the erudition of the present speaker may naturally be expected to be somewhat short of his loquacity. The allusions in this Scene have been explained in the preceding notes.

ACT 3. Sc. 3. p. 70. *The Joys of Valhalla*. "The heroes," says the Edda, " who are received into the palace of Odin, " have every day *the pleasure* of arming themselves, &c. and *of* " *cutting one another in pieces*; but as soon as the repast approaches, " they return on horseback, all safe and sound back to the Hall " of Odin, and fall to eating and drinking. Tho the number " of them cannot be counted, the flesh of the boar Serimner is " sufficient for them all; every day it is served up at table, and " every day it is renewed again intire; their beverage is beer " and mead; one single Goat, whose milk is excellent mead, " furnishes enough of that liquor to intoxicate all the heroes: " their cups are the sculls of enemies they have slain.—— " A croud of virgins wait upon the heroes, and fill their cups " as fast as they empty them." *North. Antiq. Vol. I. p. 120.*

P. 75. v. 14. *The Golden Tear*. The tears of Frea, the Goddess of love and beauty, are said to be golden; and Gold, in the language of the Scalds, is called the tears of Frea. When Balder was killed, Hela consented to restore him again to the Skies, upon condition that all the Gods should drop a tear of sorrow upon his grave. All the Deities wept, but Lok; who refused; and Hela kept her victim.

V. 20. *The Herald of thy Will*. The Handmaid Gna.

CPSIA information can be obtained at www.ICGtesting.com
Printed in the USA
LVOW111823020113

314089LV00018B/1094/P